The Bloke's Guide
to Getting Hitched

The Bloke's Guide
to Getting Hitched

Jon Smith

HAY HOUSE

Australia • Canada • Hong Kong
South Africa • United Kingdom • United States

First published and distributed in the United Kingdom by:
Hay House UK Ltd, 292B Kensal Rd, London W10 5BE.
Tel.: (44) 20 8962 1230; Fax: (44) 20 8962 1239. www.hayhouse.co.uk

Published and distributed in the United States of America by:
Hay House, Inc., PO Box 5100, Carlsbad, CA 92018-5100.
Tel.: (1) 760 431 7695 or (1) 800 654 5126;
Fax: (1) 760 431 6948 or (1) 800 650 5115. www.hayhouse.com
info@hayhouse.com

Published and distributed in Australia by:
Hay House Australia Ltd, 18/36 Ralph St, Alexandria NSW 2015.
Tel.: (61) 2 9669 4299; Fax: (61) 2 9669 4144. www.hayhouse.com.au

Published and distributed in the Republic of South Africa by:
Hay House SA (Pty), Ltd, PO Box 990, Witkoppen 2068.
Tel./Fax: (27) 11 706 6612. orders@psdprom.co.za

Published and distributed in India by:
Hay House Publishers India, Muskaan Complex, Plot No.3, B-2, Vasant Kunj,
New Delhi – 110 070. Tel.: (91) 11 41761620; Fax: (91) 11 41761630.
contact@hayhouseindia.co.in

Distributed in Canada by:
Raincoast, 9050 Shaughnessy St, Vancouver, BC V6P 6E5.
Tel.: (1) 604 323 7100; Fax: (1) 604 323 2600

© Jon Smith, 2007

The author of this book does not dispense medical advice or prescribe the use of
any technique as a form of treatment for physical or medical problems without the
advice of a physician, either directly or indirectly. The intent of the author is only
to offer information of a general nature to help you in your quest for emotional
and spiritual wellbeing. In the event you use any of the information in this book
for yourself, which is your constitutional right, the author and the publisher
assume no responsibility for your actions.

A catalogue record for this book is available from the British Library.

ISBN 978-1-4019-1546-9

Printed and bound in Great Britain by TJ International, Padstow, Cornwall.

Design by e-Digital Design.
Layout and Illustrations by Matt Windsor.

For Harrison Smith – a warm welcome
to the world, nephew

Contents

About the Author:

Despite the fashion, Jon Smith insists on remaining married to his first wife, Lisa. They have two children together. Jon writes books, screenplays and musical theatre.

An Extra Special Thanks To:

Malcolm – thanks for all your hard work, advice and counsel.

A Big Thanks To:

Rob La Francesca, Rhys Wilcox, Stephen Giles, Chris Hitchcock, Richard Burton, Neil Peters, Andy Stevens, Mick Halpin and all the other 'would-rather-remain-anonymous-husbands', both past and present, who completed the questionnaire.

Contact The Author

By Post
c/o Hay House
292b Kensal Road
London
W10 5BE
United Kingdom

By Email
jon@blokesguide.com

On The Web
www.blokesguide.com
www.justdads.co.uk

Message to the Ladies

Your partner, boyfriend, brother, uncle, dad, cousin, friend, or whoever else you had in mind when you picked up this book has no idea what he has just got himself into. I mean *no idea at all*! He's wandering around in the same old daze, unwilling and unable to ask for help and, more importantly, he has no one to turn to. Not his mates, not you, and certainly not his mum (for once!).

Marriage, it is well documented, is the ultimate commitment. And there are numerous things that need to be answered, explained or illustrated before the man who will receive this book can feel sufficiently in control to enjoy the experience.

It's not that he's deliberately being awkward, cowardly or wet about the whole wedding thing, or that he is putting up a wall of denial – at least not consciously. I mean, let's face it, he did ask you/her to marry him! It's just our reaction to anything we don't understand. Men need manuals. A + B = C. The shoulder is connected to the arm, which is connected to the wrist – straightforward, to the point and honest. *The Bloke's Guide To Getting Hitched* – no flowery prose or idealistic diatribe, no Pat dressed as Patricia in laddered tights; we want it raw and unabridged. Tell us how it is; what's the worst can happen? What's the best that can happen? If the engine is not working, what should we look at first – the alternator or the transmission?

Yes, he might be making the right noises about settling down, making an honest woman of you and dreaming of getting old with you, and he means it! But he's also scared and wants the truth, in bite-size pieces that are as easy to digest as a packet of Ritz crackers. This book tackles what *is* going on inside his head, not what *should* be going on.

This book is the product of over one hundred interviews with blokes who have lived to tell the tale – a few of whom even admitted to enjoying the experience. Let us take his hand (metaphorically, of course!) and help him on his way. He might even say thank you, and better yet, arrive in time for the wedding ... still in possession of his eyebrows and without a hangover.

Message to the Blokes

The Blokes Guide to Getting Hitched is for any man who has been thinking about popping, or who has already popped, the question. Whilst there exists a wealth of literature available to help you 'plan your *perfect* wedding', there's very little out there for us blokes in terms of dealing with the issues surrounding weddings and getting married.

If you are keen to understand the psychological changes that will occur in you, and your partner, over the next few months then this book is for you.

If you are wondering why so much fuss is being made over flower arrangements and the font size used on the invitations, then this book is for you.

If your partner handed you this book in an attempt to answer some of the questions that you keep asking her, then this book is for you.

And if you are simply keen to enjoy your wedding as much as possible, then this book is definitely for you.

Introduction

This marriage lark … What's it all about, then? Is it really possible for two people to know without doubt that they want to spend the rest of their lives together? The answer, of course, is yes – even the most hardened cynic must admit that – but marriage is also something that you will both need to work on constantly for as long as you both live (or are together). Marriage is not a static thing that starts and ends with a wedding; it's organic and constantly changing as you both get older and travel down the road that is life. Yes, there are risks, yes it will be tough, but the rewards will be truly wonderful – just be sure to go into it with both eyes open.

Choosing a wife, or to put it another way, a life partner, is a momentous life decision (and look what a mess you got into just trying to decide whether to invest in Blu-Ray or HD-DVD technology). That said, you've probably already gone ahead and done the deed ... haven't you? You have actually asked her? Or are you just toying with the idea right now?

Are You *Quite* Sure About This?!

At any rate, you're certainly thinking of getting married. And you've probably had the usual reactions: 'Good on you.' 'Brave man.' 'That takes a lot of courage.' 'We always knew you'd be the first to crack.' 'You're the marrying type.' 'You'll make a lovely couple.' 'It was obvious that you would eventually get married.'... etc.

But hold on there! Just wait a minute – just stop! Are you sure you want to be doing this? Consider the favoured position you are in right now: you probably have very few commitments, and no legally binding agreements which sign you up to some permanent relationship. You are free to do exactly as you please and you want to throw it all away! Why buy a car if you can have one on loan, or you can get the keys to any model in the showroom? DON'T BE SO STUPID!! But hey, you have probably already made your mind up. You are probably even now engaged and time is moving swiftly along towards your big day; plans are being made, decisions put in place. That's why you're reading this book, isn't it? You are just checking to see if you've missed something important off your list or seeing if you can get some inside knowledge beforehand ...

Playing Devil's Advocate ...
Well, I'd hate to be the one to throw a spanner in the works, and wouldn't dream of making light of your feelings, but are you sure? Are you really, really sure that this is what you want to do? Have you *honestly* thought this through? Have you thought about the consequences and the lifetime of

servitude that this contract might mean? Good God, man! Are you really ready to say 'No' to that sassy brunette from Accounts who approaches you, two years from now, at a work conference ... hotel room already booked ... on the company credit card ... no one will ever know ...

Okay, I am deliberately playing devil's advocate, but put it this way ... if you were buying a car, a PC or some other gadget, you'd get all the lowdown on it beforehand. You would check the cost, the specifications, assess the longevity of its use and how it might improve the way you organize your life. Alas, this often isn't quite the way with marriage. Most blokes like me, and probably like you, decide to get married in the same way we decide to buy shoes or a shirt. We walk into a shop, pick up something we like the look of, check the label to ensure it's the right size, then walk right up to the checkout. We usually don't even try it on to see if it fits. Sure, you can fool yourself that you can take it back if you don't like it, but how often does that happen? No, it sits wallowing on a clothes hanger. You might keep it, believing that you will fit back into that size sometime in the future, or that it may come in handy one day, but you know and I know that you made a mistake and are too proud to admit it. Now imagine that dreadful sense of dawning realization multiplied at least a thousand times ...

Or maybe you have been going out with someone for so long, or living together so long that you think that it won't make any difference to you if you get hitched. Well, of course it will. Marriage changes things and you should be clued up to what those changes might be before you decide to do it.

Why Bother, Anyway?

Marriage these days seems to be mostly a matter of personal preference. Couples either want to tie the knot or they don't. Although we live in a society where marriage is still very much encouraged, especially by parents and other married couples, mores and morals are always changing and now *living out of wedlock*, as the old term goes, is no longer a stigma. In fact it's rather commonplace. Even the Church of England is becoming more flexible on the idea. Sure, I expect 'shotgun weddings' happen every day of the week, but generally approaches to getting married have changed. Marriage still has its legal, religious and societal overtones, but, when questioned, brides and grooms often answer that they are getting married as a public show of commitment, or as a precursor to having children, or increasingly after having them, or for basic tax or legal reasons, or sometimes even because they just fancied an excuse to hold a big party. And what with Civil Partnerships for gay and lesbian couples, it seems that everybody is getting in on the act.

This book may be written for heterosexual couples but in fact all the information here is just as valid for gay couples too. And that considered, perhaps one of the best approaches to modern marriage is to see it as a happy celebration of commitment, a public demonstration of your future partnership.

The Benefits Of Being Married

Back in the good old days there was also a financial benefit to being married, in the form of Married Persons' Tax Allowance. This has now, essentially, disappeared (unless you're over 75, which isn't really going to help you at the moment...) Nowadays, financially speaking, the benefits of being married are a little less tangible, but there are benefits in a number of other areas. Obviously it improves your sense of personal wellbeing and can be a real tonic for all those male insecurities. Then there's the knowledge that no matter how hard a day you've had, no matter how badly Liverpool lost to Man Utd, you know that you will be able to go home and be with your wife, the woman who has chosen you over all other men, and tell her all about it. Granted, that isn't going to mean you're any better off financially every month, but it counts towards something.

There's a respect that comes from being married. You may find new possibilities open up in terms of raising finance, in the form of loans from the bank or new credit cards. You might also be treated a little differently during the next round of promotions at work. This treatment can be intangible, but it's certainly there under the surface.

Marriage is an incredibly rewarding partnership that allows two people to completely and unconditionally trust each other. Very soon you will have a wife to share in all your trials and tribulations. When a marriage works, it works very well. It also feels nice to be married, and whether we admit to it or not, us blokes *are* insecure at the best of times. Marriage brings security.

What's In It For Me?
Do you really, honestly, know what marriage actually entails? Sure, your Mum and Dad may be married, or were once; but you wouldn't start wearing cardigans or decide to take up golf just because they did. Whether or not to get married is one of the biggest decisions of your life, so, at the risk of sounding like your old headmaster, you need to think long and hard about what you're doing. Look at it long-term. Consider the consequences. Analyze the plans. This book is mainly about the choices you will have to

make regarding the practicalities of the wedding itself. But I also want to think about the whys and wherefores of getting married. Neither I, nor any of the husbands interviewed for this book, are relationship counsellors and I can't tell you whether or not you are making the right choice – only you, deep down, will ever know that. All I aim to do is to give you some insider knowledge, a few tips to the wise, and maybe even a few laughs along the way (precious few of those around, sadly, when the wedding plans get really serious). But first and foremost I'd like to make you think about marriage, about (oh please, Lord, no –) commitment, about your future and about why it is so important to get things right.

What's In It For Her?

Which brings us to point one. Have you ever considered why she wants to marry you anyway? No, seriously, have you? You may believe that you look like Brad Pitt on one of his good days, and possess the charm of James Bond. You may even be extremely rich and successful, talented and dynamic, with a heart to match the size of your wallet. But let's be honest. Like me, you are probably a fairly average guy with a fairly average job and that's about it. She could have chosen a lot of blokes; she chose you. Did she just end up with you by chance or was there some magnetic, strangely mystical force at work? Or is there a deeply Freudian reason why you get to be Mr Lucky? You may be in for some surprises ...

Guess what? A lot of it is down to biology and evolution. Women, like other primates, have their own mating strategies [1]. First they like healthy guys. Okay, some emaciated, drug-addled loser may be all over the papers for getting into some supermodel's knickers recently, but generally women like healthier males. Health, happiness and reproduction tend to go hand-in-hand. Women also like blokes who look fairly normal facially, so if on one side of your face you look like Gonzo from the *Muppets,* and on the other you look like fat Dave from down the pub, you are going to have your work cut out. They also like their future mate to have access to resources ... err ... okay, in the 21st century that roughly translates as wealth. Yes, it's a shocker, but women like ambitious, successful men. The good news is that this does not mean that you have to be rich and successful when you get together, just that it is desirable that you have the potential to be so in the future.

It is also said that women prefer men who are, in their eyes, of an equal if not a higher status. This ensures not only that they will be treated better in society, but that any future offspring will be too. Older and bigger (broad shoulders) are also good too, as are age and maturity, which are seen as important. So somewhere in their hard-wire programming, women have something that says wealthy, high-status, big, brawny males are the business – but come on, you knew that already. (How else do all those ageing old gits manage to walk around with beautiful trophy wives?) So it's all hunter-gatherer stuff, then? Well, not quite.

The way we choose a partner is actually much more complex than whether or not you can wrestle a tiger or happen to be a very wealthy businessman. There are other influences at work which relate to upbringing, class, outlook, geography and shared interests – which is why not every female wants to marry a tall, rich ex-footballer from Scotland. That we choose people from our peer group and age and background means we have many different options. Nevertheless, you can bet all those age-old elements are still there in the background. If she has chosen you, it is because you fit into some sort of mental and social template she has. (And as blokes, we know that there are those other rules of attraction that also apply, like the fact that you really enjoy being together or the fact of her having really big breasts...)

Basically, she has picked you because she thinks you are right for her. And maybe you just have to trust her on that one. If there's that old adage 'She could have done better' hanging around your head, it probably relates to what you imagine others' expectations to be, rather than what she sees in you. She has chosen you for a host of reasons and that's what makes you special to her and that's all that matters. That said, it should also be remembered that if five years down the line of married life, you turn your back on a promising career in a small law firm and become an alcohol-addicted couch potato working as a part-time shopping centre security guard, you may be for the push.

Why Do You Want To Marry Her?

Okay, it's your turn now for the evolutionary caveman claptrap. According to some eminent social scientists, blokes choose women on ... YOU ARE ALL SO SHALLOW ... oh yes, you know it already: looks. Blokes also have that caveman instinct deep down, and fertility and faithfulness are all wrapped up in there somewhere too. Hip-to-waist ratio, childbearing hips, an hourglass figure ... youth. It is all so predictable: we like young, fertile women. Women know this and that's one of the reasons for all that female investment in make-up. It's all to do with sexual overtones ('Hey, red lips, I like that, it's sexy'), and sex and fertility and youthful looks are all bound up together.

Anyway, the reason I'm banging on about all this is that it does have repercussions for the potential happiness of your marriage. What are your plans long-term? If she's partly choosing you for your earnings potential and security and you're choosing her for her fertility, it's reasonable to expect you to have some realistic discussions about what, exactly, you both want from the deal.

Apparently, the faithful element is particularly important too. Blokes are basically fundamentally insecure. They worry that their future partners may be about to be impregnated by some other alpha male they meet at the office. Men feel the urge to sleep around themselves, and know that other blokes feel (and sometimes act on) that urge too. So there is always something edgy and suspicious in the old male psyche. This is why, in our mature 21st-century, women are still susceptible to accusations of promiscuity. This is why men get the 'He looks just like his Dad' stuff when a baby is born – it's reassurance for us. Men are attracted to women who flirt, as long as they don't flirt too much and they don't flirt with everyone. They like women to be successful, but not too successful. And one thing blokes really can't stand is when women show them up, in terms of competition or in their relations with their mates. Us blokes are basically very sad and very insecure.

But Enough Of The Theory ...

If someone were to ask you, however, why you felt attracted to your future wife, the old hunter-gatherer theory wouldn't even come into it. In spite of the fact that blokes hate all that chick-lit romance stuff and only admit to crying when Liverpool FC come back from 3-0 down to win the Champions' League Final (love it!), blokes often describe their reasons for marrying in the most romantic and emotional terms. They even use the word LOVE. So there is something more behind the wish to marry other than finding a younger replacement for Mum to do the laundry and the washing-up. Terms like *partnership* and *companionship* are key. In spite of the urge to sow our wild oats, there seems to be a need to build a genuine and hopefully stable unit around oneself; to become a couple. And of course there is the matter of children. It may be something that you personally, or both of you, have decided you don't want to do, but if you do and when it happens, it can be a seismic shift in a relationship, changing the old rules of wedded bliss and establishing new emotional bonds and commitment.

Being 'In Love'

However, now that we've openly used the 'L' word, I'd like to sound a note of caution. Basically, people who are madly in love are simply not rational about much, and somewhere mixed in with all that lust, love, possessiveness, commitment and conflict, it is easy to decide to get the marriage thing wrong. It is not surprising to find that psychologists are still debating the effect of emotions on decision making. It can all be a bit frightening, but try and think back to some of the people you have had relationships with or some of the times when you were 'in love' in the past. It probably won't take long to also remember the 'Why did I ever go out with them?' stage, or that classic row in a Chinese take-away! What would have happened if you hadn't come to your senses! Love is a form or infatuation. It's an 'I must have' mentality; it takes possession of your rational thought. You bore your mates, you ignore your mates, and you make all sorts of stupid decisions.

You've probably seen for yourself the 'Why is he marrying her?' situation. One of my friends introduced me to his fiancée. He is an extroverted, charismatic party animal and an academic at a big university. A big drinker with a big intellect who had a string of relationships with some really interesting and attractive women, and yet here he was preparing to marry a woman with no discernable social graces, who seemed to be bad-humoured, bad-tempered, vindictive, petty and controlling, and who was none too bright either. Why did they get married? Well, they were 'in love'. Or at least they thought they were. Loving your future partner is of course a necessity, but rushing into marriage when you are still at that blind-to-any-faults honeymoon stage is probably not a good idea. That said, one of my respondents met a girl at a party, went out for six weeks, then walked into Chelsea Registry Office and got hitched. They are still together and still very happy.

My Mum And Dad Would Really Like It If ...

There are also many external factors which can influence couples to make the leap. We know that parents can sometimes object to marriages, but it is equally true that couples still get engaged and married because 'Their parents want them to' or because 'Their grandparents don't like them living together in an unholy alliance'. One of my friends even got engaged as his grandfather was dying because the couple wanted to celebrate it with him – admirable but not the best way to make such a weighty decision. Religion may play a part in this too, as sometimes one or both of the couple feels the need to follow the conventions of their upbringing. Other influences can be the wish to emigrate, or to stay in a country. One of the classics is of course pregnancy – oh yes, don't believe that everyone will be okay with you being parents and unmarried. There are also legal reasons, even peer pressure. Whatever external factors you feel are influencing you, just make sure they are only *one* of the reasons, and not *the* reason for getting hitched.

External factors must be judged as secondary. It sounds so obvious but is still worth reiterating: your reasons for getting married should always be that you really want to spend your life with the person you have chosen. If you allow external pressures to influence or drive your decisions, you could end up in a much bigger mess down the line. When you draw up a balance sheet of why you want to get married, external factors must be put in perspective. If you find that it is only external factors that are making you want to marry, then don't do it.

Marriage As Metamorphosis?
Equally, it is foolish to think that getting married will somehow magically transform your life or your relationship with your partner. It's not just women who get carried away by the idealistic fantasy of being married. Don't ignore the danger signs. If your partner irritates you on a daily basis; if your sexual relations aren't what they once were; if you are terrible at organizing your finances and, in fact, pretty terrible at organization generally – these problems won't simply go away when you get married. If anything, they will become amplified – and you will be in a far worse position, in terms of rectifying them, after the marriage than before. Marriage is not a fix-all. It might remove the long faces in your house all the way from now to the honeymoon – there will simply be too much to organize between now and then to have time to be angry – but what it won't do is solve any deep-rooted problems between you; if anything, it is only going to make them worse.

Marriage As A Sticking Plaster
Unfortunately, one of the worst possible engagement scenarios is also one of the most common. This is when a

couple have been together for a long time and the relationship is in a state of stagnation, with problems never really being resolved, so they decide that the way to change things is to get married. This is, of course, completely *mad*, but all too common. Getting married to hold things together may work sometimes. Marriage does bind couples together and make it difficult for them to walk away. But it will not be a magical solution to any problems; in the relationship and though the marriage may hold you together in the short time, with all the rush and bustle of wedding planning, the problems will inevitably reappear in future. If you are willing to go through all the stresses and strains of planning a wedding, then you could do the far simpler thing of going to see a relationship counsellor. The local council service can provide you with the contact numbers, or see the generic number at the end of this book. All you have to do is keep an evening free a week for a couple of months. There is nothing wrong with doing it. You haven't failed. If you can't fix your car, you take it to a specialist, and that's all you are doing here. Long-term relationships often have stresses and strains and you would be surprised how much of a relief it is to talk to an expert about it. It really does work and clear the air. So get your relationship sorted out before you even think about getting married.

Mr On-The-Rebound
Equally, make sure that your reasons for getting married are not to do with the insecurities or passions of an earlier relationship. Another terrible scenario is Mr or Ms Rebound. Getting married on the rebound: we hear about it all the time. Rushing from one relationship to another is very popular, we all seem to be serial monogamists these days, but it is not good to top it off with marriage. If a partner has baggage (or haulage) then they should sort it

out beforehand. (I say, again, sort your relationship out before you even think about getting married.) The rebound factor often comes into play when a bloke is nearing the end of his shelf life as a handsome young stud and a woman is hearing that old biological clock ticking away for dear life. This may not be so terrible, as many a relationship is based on compromise and some form of long-term arrangement, but it is definitely something to be worried about. If you have just come out of a relationship, you will be very insecure. You will probably have been trying to drink yourself stupid every night and may have tried to sleep with everything with a pulse. You can be so relieved when you finally find another girlfriend that you mistake relief for love. My advice to blokes out there is not to rush. Don't panic.

Age Cannot Wither Her, Nor Custom Stale Her Infinite Variety ...

Age is also something that should be considered when getting married. If you are thinking about running off together and getting married at sixteen, then you are almost certainly making a whopper of a mistake. Okay, we all know people who have got married at twenty-one and are happy and still together fifty years on, but even these people can have regrets. People who have dated since school, married early, and have not had any other relationships often express regret that they did not go out with other people or have more sexual experiences. This regret may be minor, but it reflects a wider realization that they both would have benefited personally from a few more emotional experiences before they became committed to one person.

Couples are getting married later these days, but

not that much later. Not so long ago the average person got married in their late 20s; now they do it in their early 30s. This is a reflection of the greater personal freedom we have now in our relationships, as well as different social expectations and the desire for financial stability. But it is also true that getting married very early is just not that popular any more. If you are a mature person, if you have experienced life (please don't say *sown your wild oats!*), you will have a much better perspective on the type of relationship you want in the long term. People change. You may remember the film *Educating Rita*, where the central character only discovers the person she *really* is later on in life, through education. But in doing so she also moves away emotionally from the husband she married when she was young. I mention it because it's a classic scenario. Give yourself some time to have fun and to grow up first. Really, what's the big rush?

Big age differences between couples should also be considered. I'm not just talking about those 20-year-old blokes who marry a 60-year-old dowager, in some mad, Freudian, thought-provoking news story. Just take into account that if you are 60 and your wife is 20 (and probably marrying you for your money – sorry, mate), in ten years' time she is still going to be a good-looking woman and you are going to be very wrinkly indeed. It may work, but it is a risk. Then there is the much more common scenario of the 35-year-old who is marrying someone who is much younger, say 19. It may not sound like that much of an age difference but the 35-year-old will probably be coming home from work, wanting to relax, while the 19-year-old is coming home from lectures and wanting to go to an all-night rave. It's about being at different stages in life. Where there is a major discrepancy between outlooks and expectations – and not just in terms of age – this can break a couple apart. If you are relatively close in age your outlooks and expectations are likely to be more similar. You may not remember all the same TV programmes and you may not have the same taste in music, but it will at least be familiar territory.

Having said all that, ultimately it is about how you get along. If you are aware of the differences, you can plan for them and adjust your life around them.

Checking Your 'Sell-by' Date

However, it is certainly true that as the bloke's pulling 'shelf life' is nearing its end, and as the female of the species's body clock is ticking away for dear life, marriage seems to become a much simpler decision. You have done your dating, you have been chucked once too often, you have had your heart broken. You have woken up with someone you don't fancy, gone out with someone for ages, then found out you don't really work together; you have even done your time stomping around the pubs and nightclubs with a large placard saying 'I am desperate'. Finally, you find yourself in a relationship with someone you do get along with and hey presto, it all seems suddenly clear! It's simpler for her too. You are (we hope) no longer the one-track-minded, sexually-fixated, drink-filled lad. You have had some of your rough edges knocked off and you may actually even be good company. Okay, you are probably still a sports-mad boy at heart with an unhealthy fixation on electrical gadgets, the major battles of World War II and beer. But you are also now in the zone of possible husband – even Dad – material.

How Big Can A Really Big Mistake Be?

Whatever your reasons, you need to remember that this is one of the most serious and important decisions any person will ever have to make in their life. (A decision that also impacts on two sets of families and friends, not to mention any existing, or future children.) That means that if it's not the right decision, you are making a big, big, big, big mistake and creating an ever bigger, deeper, smellier mess. Just because it is a joint decision doesn't mean it's the right decision.

If you get it wrong you will either end up serving time in an unhappy marriage, or end up getting DIVORCED, which is not a word we want to use too often in this book. And with all that comes all the fallout between respective families, not to mention the impact that would have on any children you may have had in the meantime. So, loathe as I am to be the purveyor of doom, it pays to know your facts.

According to the latest UK figures, nearly 40 per cent of all marriages end in divorce. The most recent figures show that almost 170,000 people divorced in 2004. However, 'Over the last 10 years the average age at divorce in England and Wales has risen from 39.6 to 43.1 years for men and from 37.0 to 40.6 years for women.' Divorce is especially on the increase among people who have been married before. The good news is that 'Divorce rates for men and women under 40 have fallen most steeply.' However, lads, in 53 per cent of divorces it was the husband's behaviour that was cited as the main reason for the break-up. Oh yes, boys, we have been caught playing around. We have been rumbled for getting drunk and spending all the family cash, for being a bloody useless article and a host of other things, all of which has prompted our wives to show us the door. So before you even think of getting married, remember that if you do you will no longer be a SINGLE BLOKE afterwards and *you will have to change your behaviour.*

Anything Could Happen
And maybe you'll have to change in quite drastic ways ...

Imagine this: You have been happily married for four years, you are both in your early thirties and you receive a call from the hospital. Your wife has been in an accident. She is alive, but she will never be able to walk again.

Imagine this: Your wife returns to work after bringing up your two children for ten years. She lands a role with a large blue-chip company that means she is abroad for two weeks every month. The salary is superb but it means that you have to leave your professional role after fifteen years to look after your children and become a full-time homemaker.

Imagine this: You are happily married for fifty years and your wife, the mother of your four children and grandmother of seven, dies peacefully in her sleep, aged 79. You outlive her for sixteen years, refusing to leave the marital home or to remove her clothes from the wardrobe.

The marriage that you are contemplating will end, one way or another, some day. How it ends, by and large, will be beyond your control. You are proposing to marry someone: for richer for poorer, in sickness and in health, until you are *dead*. Maybe this all sounds a bit morbid but I just wanted to emphasize that that's how serious this statement of intent really is.

... Still With Me?

So, after all that you're still with me? Fair enough. You're either lying or you really are committed ... let's hope it's the latter and, having got the unpleasant lecture out of the way, let's move swiftly on.

Whatever the reasons for choosing your partner – you're mates; you like redheads; she is wealthy and goes like a steam train – you have also chosen her because *she is special to you*. That is something that should be remembered, especially as the wedding planning is, for most blokes, an ordeal of *The Lord Of The Rings* proportions. All right, maybe not that bad, but you will certainly encounter plenty of rings, monsters and temptations ...

The Engagement

Rings, proposals,
parties and pre-nups

The first thing to remember about getting engaged is that
although you will be not be signing the contract of
marriage until the actual wedding, getting engaged is
tantamount to getting married. You are asking your partner
to become your wife; be a mother to your children; even
to bury you (hopefully) in years to come. Somewhere in
between jetting off on your honeymoon and dying, you will
attend family funerals, argue, fight, care for each other,
enjoy holidays, sleep in separate rooms, sleep with each
other, possibly procreate, and visit Accident and Emergency
at least once. Your wife will have to endure all of your
present shortcomings and many more that are still to
materialize. You will have to endure hers. At times your
marriage will stretch your emotions to near breaking point.
At others, it will be the most rewarding union you will have
with another human being. You are proposing a

partnership that theoretically only Mother Nature (or your gods) should be able to put asunder. In short, the most important decision you will ever make.

The De-Valuing Of Engagement

Young people get engaged a lot, often because they don't know what to say to each other any more. Maybe it happened to you or maybe it happened to someone you know, but there's a temptation within many of us to pop the question at a very early age – perhaps this girl is your first love, or your mates have already done it so you feel you need to catch up, or you are so determined to get a hand down her knickers that you'll say anything for that first touch … Whatever the reason, chances are you've moved on and you are no longer in contact with your first 'fiancée'. A few years older and hopefully wiser, this time you're going to make sure you do this right … This time you are doing it for real.

Work On The Assumption That She'll Say 'Yes'

Getting engaged for many love-struck males can simply be a handy thing to say, at a certain moment in time. And sometimes that is fine. If that moment happens to be after a heavy night on the Stella, by telephone, to an incredibly angry partner who expected you home two hours ago, then that particular time is probably not a good idea. If you and your partner have been enduring months or years of bickering, with arguments constantly reappearing and refusing to be resolved, then it is also probably not a good idea. However, New Year's Eve parties are a classic time for proposals, as are romantic beach walks whilst on holiday. Romantic meals for two and surprise public displays of affection also rank highly in the nation's favourites. But fundamentally there are no good or bad places to propose. Doing it on New Year's Eve doesn't make it any more or any less important than doing it in mid-September – it's the impetus for the proposal that has to be sound. The venue and timing are almost irrelevant.

The important thing is that proposing to someone should really mean you want to get married – not stay engaged for evermore. By all means set a date for a couple of years in the future (you will probably need that long to save up for the Mongolian mounted archers she wants to build the silk marquee) but set a date (or at least a month) and try your very best to stick to it. Don't get engaged to make up for your recent behaviour and put a smile on her face, or as an excuse to try and get more jiggy – get engaged to be married. Mean it.

I Did It My Way
If we accept that the actual wedding day is very much the bride's day, then we should try to ensure that the marriage proposal is very much the bloke's day. But that doesn't mean that you will necessarily enjoy it in any way. More often than not, the planning, organization and eventual delivery of the words 'Will you marry me?' are something we do secretly and without consultation. More often than not, even the lucky lady in question doesn't get a warning. All the angst surrounding choosing a ring, picking the moment, keeping it all under wraps and then executing the plan pretty much mean that the wedding itself is a breeze in comparison. Your future wife would probably forgive you for seeming apparently uninterested in what colour napkins should be on each table if she fully understood the sheer terror and worry you went through when you were first assessing whether or not she would say 'yes'. In comparison to this near heart-attack-inducing experience, the fruit content of the wedding cake pales into insignificance.

Choosing A Ring

Before we get to the nitty-gritty of the actual proposal, we have more material matters to attend to. Now, I'm guessing here you don't spend a lot of time in jewellers'. Who does? In fact, I would also wager that the last time you bought a ring was when you fell head over heels in love with the girl who first kissed you in the local park, and you went out and splashed one month's pocket money on a heart-shaped locket you spotted in the Argos catalogue ... and then she dumped you for a third-year with a deeper voice. Well, I'm afraid you're going to have to spend a little more than £15 this time round. A whole lot more. In fact, if you're a traditional sort of chap, you should be looking to spend one month's salary (not sure if that's net or gross and it's certainly not tax-deductible) on a band of metal with a diamond stuck on the top. And remember, it may be just a bit of metal to you, but to her and the rest of the world it is a symbol of the eternity you intend to spend together.

The biggest decision you will need to make regarding the ring is whether or not you are letting your future fiancée in on the proceedings, and therefore essentially proposing to her without a ring to offer, or whether you're going to throw caution to the wind, 'borrow' one of her rings and take your hairy self off to a jeweller's to buy a ring in secret. Neither decision is any less admirable, but the 'unexpected' proposal is certainly the most traditional and romantic – however, having your partner there with you in the shop will ensure that you buy the right ring (she is bound to have strong views on this) and buy it in the right size.

You will also need to have a think about whether or not you want to wear an engagement ring too. It is quite common for men to buy their wedding ring at this stage and wear it throughout the engagement and the marriage.

Equally, you can decide not to bother with an engagement ring but to wear a wedding ring, once you are married. Or you can decide not to wear a ring at all, because they're for girls … it's up to you. I am not a huge fan of rings but wanted a wedding ring and surprised myself at just how quickly I got used to the initially alien feeling of having a bit of metal in between my fingers. Unfortunately, I got so used to it I wouldn't realize when the ring had in fact slipped off, or when my finger had turned blue as the size of my finger ebbed and flowed depending on the weather or how hydrated I was on that particular day. In the end, after a very bizarre experience involving apparently losing the ring in a compacter then having it returned to me (amazingly), I put it away in a drawer until I could get it resized. That was over two years ago … maybe I should have gone for the posh silver cufflinks instead?

Rings aren't cheap and if you're planning to buy two, they're going to make a large dent in your savings account. Do consider buying second-hand or antique rings as a viable alternative – if your bride-to-be is into the vintage look you won't be scorned as a cheapskate and with a professional clean the rings can look as good as they did when they were made. It's an option.

Asking Her Father

One of the old traditions is, of course, asking her dad for his daughter's hand in marriage. The very thought of this can induce severe bowel movement in the bloke that has to do it. And it's certainly not a prerequisite any more, but it is a great way to impress the in-laws and ensure that they put their hand into their pocket towards the cost of the wedding. Asking Pops for his approval will obviously be easier if he has met you, at least once, before you ask the question, and more so, if the one time he met you before wasn't when he interrupted you having your wicked way with his daughter on their new leather sofa. Whatever the case, you might want to take him out for a quiet pint, away from the rest of the family, to ensure that your well-prepared speech isn't lost to Tiger Woods getting a birdie at St Andrews or whatever else could be possibly more important to him than you admitting to having defiled his daughter.

It is just a formality nowadays, but this is the perfect opportunity to establish a good ongoing working relationship with your in-laws, so you'd be wise to treat it seriously. Very, very seriously. You may think your girlfriend's dad likes you and he may, but he probably liked her last boyfriend too. It is supposedly a courtesy, but in fact it is likely to be the first serious dealings and negotiations you are going to have with your future father-in-law. He may be really happy for you both, but it is still a delicate matter – we are talking about his daughter, for crying out loud. Your genes are probably going to be mixed with his. You are the new male ape in his household. If she were your daughter, how would you like to be treated?

Asking or telling her father (even if you have actually asked the girl in question already) is still something that should be done in a fairly intimate situation. You should be ready at least to be able to discuss any plans that you have made with your girlfriend. You should also try to include her mother and maybe signal to her siblings that something big is afoot. What's more, you can use the occasion as a guide to how to deal with difficult matters in future, as it is unlikely that you will know her parents that well or have had serious dealings with them before. Once the wedding plans get into full swing, you will have many more such serious discussions, I can tell you.

What If They Don't Approve?

Don't presume that her parents are going to be completely over the moon with delight. They may be happy, but they will also be concerned. And there is always the possibility that they will object to you, or question your actions. One interviewee reported that when he first proposed to his wife, he was unemployed and generally dossing about, travelling and doing part-time jobs. Her father asked him, in no uncertain terms, how he intended to support his daughter and what future he thought he had. Another respondent to the questionnaire told how his future mother-in-law was clearly absolutely horrified at the prospect of him marrying her daughter and made that quite clear from the outset. Time changes and time heals and in both of these cases the problems were resolved, after a fashion. But it is also possible that the parents may object very strongly and, in these cases, you will have to sit down with your girlfriend and consider your options.

In cases where parents do object you have three choices. They are: to go ahead anyway, to call it off and split up, or to call it off and stay together in the hope that time may present a solution. Objections can be fundamental. A work acquaintance told me that he had problems not with the parents, but with the grandparents. He is black and from Uganda and they took exception. Apparently now that they have children and thus there are grandchildren, he has finally been accepted, but it was very hard for the couple for a number of years. In other cases, religious or social barriers can overshadow engagements. Even in this day and age, a daughter wanting to marry someone who is from a lower social class or different social background can make things awkward. In the end though, it is your choice and it is your life. Don't be afraid of conflict and stand up for what you want. You are going to have to do that a lot over the years, anyway – it's called being part of a family.

The Proposal

We all know the etiquette for proposals of marriage. The expected rituals could come straight out of a Victorian melodrama. After a period of courtship, where the couple get to know each other, the bloke is supposed to take the lead. He is so sure that he is going to get the 'YES' answer, when the proposal is made, that he asks the father for his daughter's hand (a very odd phrase, if you ask me!). Then, after a few deep and sensible questions, the father gives his assent. The mother of the future bride is absolutely delighted. And then, basically, he goes back to the female in question, gets down on one knee and tells her she's a lucky girl. From there it moves swiftly on to the wedding and they live happily ever after. Ummm... well, that is fiction, unfortunately, and what is more, we are all well aware from all that *Jane Eyre* and *Pride and Prejudice* stuff that it wasn't like that then and it isn't going to be like that now.

The modern proposal is of course a very different matter, but it still has all those historical resonances of love, commitment and family. Just because many couples never bother to get married, engaged or otherwise, does not mean that the wedding proposal has lost all of its significance. Getting engaged is a really big step.

By rights, it should be simple; you ask her, she says yes. You both discuss getting engaged and decide to get married. A typical engagement is described here, by Simon:

We had both discussed the possibility of getting married but we had not formally decided to get engaged. I suppose it is fair to say that it was on the agenda. On a visit to her parents, we decided to tell them, and kind of ask her father at the same time, but it was more of an announcement. We then told our friends, when we saw them, but there was no big announcement or engagement party. It was just part of our everyday life, really; a natural move forward.

But the romantic proposal, the surprise proposal, is still alive and kicking. One person from my survey booked a holiday in the Maldives for him and his girlfriend, spoke with the parents, even booked extra days' holiday with her work without her knowledge, and after they had flown out, he proposed on the beach at sunset with champagne on ice – oh, and she said 'yes'. But she did say that she had suspected that he was going to propose and she would have been very displeased if he hadn't. So remember, there are still choices for how a bloke makes a proposal of marriage. The only way to judge, really, is to base your choice upon what you hope your partner would like.

The only word of warning is to be sure in your head that you actually want to do this in the first place. It is possible to keep the romantic element and still be pragmatic. Have a joint agreement before a 'surprise' engagement. Being able to make the decision to get married because you *want* to, instead of because you *have* to, with all the freedom and flexibility that implies, just goes to show how we have progressed in the modern day.

Some examples of proposals for you – either to give you some inspiration, or so that you know how you don't want to do it!

Rhys: *It was our third anniversary and we were living in London. We had a meal at Smollensky's on The Strand and I apologized profusely for not getting her a present. We got the tube to Tower Hill and walked across the bridge. When we got to the middle I told her that I had been lying. She was very nervous. I said I had got her something and pulled out the little box. She started blubbing. My work was done.*

Jon: *My partner and our daughter were away in France on holiday. I was in the house surrounded by women's clothes and children's toys, but no one to use them. I felt like I had been abandoned and decided, despite being vehemently anti-marriage for so long, that I had changed my mind. I couldn't wait until they got home to ask, so I proposed via a long-distance phone call. She said yes and we celebrated properly on her return.*

Rob: *Barbados on holiday. Problem is I had an expensive ring in my hand luggage and we get to check-in and they say "Your bag is too heavy for hand luggage – it can't go on as hand luggage," to which I'm thinking there's no way a £1600 ring (obtained from a mate for £600!!) is leaving my sight. Massive scene later – I'm checked in with ring safely in hand luggage (emptied half the contents into my main luggage whilst swearing in Italian under my breath, with a long queue of impatient fellow passengers tutting behind me!). First night on holiday; had a wonderful evening, we were a little drunk on the balcony under a beautiful starlit sky and I read out some words I'd written for the moment and popped the question. We both then ran downstairs, took our clothes off and skinny-dipped in the hotel pool.*

Stephen: *By saying 'How about it, then?' in a hotel room in Bruges, while watching* Noel's House Party *and drinking champagne from the bottle.*

Neil: *By international fax to Italy where Emma was working, as I'd been sailing in UAE and Europe.*

Andy: *I booked a table in a restaurant for Sunday lunchtime and had bought a ring in the meantime. On the way to the restaurant I pulled the car over by the beach and asked her if she wanted to marry me. She burst into tears, which I wasn't sure was a compliment or not at the time. We then went for a nice meal and told everyone afterwards.*

All Say 'Aaaahhh ...'

Now that she has accepted your proposal, you are engaged to be married. Pretty cool, hey? Although everything is leading towards the big day, it is important not to wish the engagement away as quickly as possible. Even if you have been cohabiting for many years, this is your dress rehearsal for marriage. If things are shaky, tempers frayed and everything has gone horribly wrong in the bedroom department, then all of these issues aren't going to magically disappear the moment that you exchange wedding vows. Far from it. Use the engagement, no matter how long, to perfect the relationship as best you can. Iron out the difficulties and the differences to ensure that you are both going into this marriage in as strong a position as possible.

But Wait ... What If She Says No?

Letting a guy down gently is a lovely euphemism for ritual humiliation. You have asked her to marry you and she has said no. What could be worse? Excuse me, but were you drunk? Yes, that is right. Did you, by any chance, go out with your mates, have lots and lots of beer and then ring her up at her parent's house at two in the morning and drool and slur down the phone that you want her to marry you? Or did you sort of bring it up like, 'Do you want to buy a fish tank/do you want to get married?'

Come on, mate, be serious. If you are going to ask your girlfriend to marry you, then do it properly. Women take marriage very seriously. They may say no because they don't think you are being serious enough. It could be that they want to spend the rest of their life with you, but don't want to get married. It may be that they like you very, very much but they are not ready for the commitment at that time and want to wait. Okay, it may be that they actually don't want to marry you because you are bit of a tool and they want out. But if you do ask her seriously and she does say no, seriously, then you are in for a very big 'our joint future' style chat. Being too heavy or too keen in a girlfriend's eyes is BAD.

Start Spreading The News ...

So, I'm assuming she is going to say, or has said, yes. Great! What next? Well, as if you needed any prompting, you had better announce your good news to the world. You may or may not have asked her father for her hand. If you haven't, then the first people to hear about your plans should always be your own children, if you have any, and then both your own and your fiancée's parents. That starts the whole chain reaction – obviously you'll get round to telling uncles, aunties, cousins and grandparents, but rest assured your mum will be well on the case the moment you tell her, so leave all of them on the back burner and get on with telling your siblings and friends.

On this one occasion you'll be very pleased that blokes are blokes – your mates will wish you well and might even inquire about possible dates for the wedding, then they'll leave it at that. (Although they're not really interested in details at this stage, you have inadvertently just started advertising for the role of best man, and therefore your mates are beginning a subtle series of machinations to show themselves off in the best light, whilst trying to appear aloof about the subject.) Your fiancée, however, will find telling friends far more laborious as she recounts, in minute detail, the exact location, emotion and words used during the proposal, coupled with a level of professionalism and knowledge, when describing the ring, that would shame an *Antiques Roadshow* expert. These conversations will take hours, so you're better off using your mobile to tell your mates and then taking yourself off for two days – because when you come back, she'll still be on the phone.

If it's at all possible, have the engagement party (if you're having one) arranged, or at least a date decided upon when you ring to announce the engagement; that way you'll save yourselves tonnes more phone calls.

Hitting Her With Both Barrels

Meanwhile, you will have some serious legal matters to contend with. One hundred years ago it was unthinkable that your wife would not take on your family name as her own. This was simply how things were done (along with child-labour, dreadful working conditions, women not being able to vote, and so on.) Thankfully, it is much more common now for women *not* to adopt their husband's family name if they do not wish, or for both parties to adopt a double-barreled name. The latter does make for the ultimate in true partnership, but can create some silly combinations – Smith-Jones, Smiley-Pratt, Small-Bucket etc. Once again, it is a subject best brought out into the open very early on. One of the parties may in fact have very strong views and the other not be bothered in the slightest. Only by addressing the issue very early on will you be able to come to an agreement that is truly a combined choice and not a dictated peace.

Decide all this pretty soon after you propose – if for no other reason than people are going to ask, and it would look pretty silly if you didn't know the answer. Don't forget, if you have a daft name (like Smith, for example) you could always change your name to hers ... but as this is not an automatic marital right you will need to go through the deed-poll process to make it legally recognized.

What About A Pre-Nup?

A prenuptial agreement is a contract signed by couples before they get married that essentially highlights how the couple's assets would be divided if the marriage should fail. They were originally designed to protect high-net-worth individuals from marrying someone (read 'pauper'), only to lose half of everything when he or she requested a divorce six months down the line. If you hadn't guessed, they first appeared in the US and are used regularly there. Currently, prenuptial agreements are not legally binding in England and Wales, so they're not really worth the paper they're written on – although there is always the chance that the law may be changed and may acknowledge existing pre-nups retrospectively.

The major problem with pre-nups, as many people see it, is that if one party is even contemplating the idea, then they are:

a: not 100 per cent committed to the relationship in the first place, or

b: they don't trust their partner's motives 100 per cent and feel they need some protection.

If either of these is the case, then there is going to be a certain amount of suspicion and resentment well before the couple have even decided on a venue for the wedding. However, a realist would argue that many people consider pre-nups even when they are committed whole-heartedly, it's just that none of us knows quite what is round the corner. And you could say that if two people decide to get married, it is because they love each other as people, not for the size of their wallet, and a pre-nup actually clarifies that – 'If you are prepared to marry me even though you know you definitely won't be getting your hands on my millions if should we break up, you must really love me.'

Think Of It Like A Contract

If I were to play devil's advocate, then I would argue that, for instance, when we take on a new role in a company we always face the prospect of redundancy, being sacked or deciding to leave in the future – this obviously isn't the intention of either the employer or the employee, but who knows what circumstances may occur further down the line? The prospect of job termination has to be incorporated into your contract of employment. From the day you begin employment you have a clear understanding of what will happen, financially, if your role as employee (or *husband* or *wife*) terminates. You feel more secure in the knowledge, and the employer feels more secure. You may end up working for that company for the next forty years with never a bad word said. You may end up not pleasing and satisfying your employer any more and you are sent away. Or you may meet a younger, more vibrant, more exciting company hungry for your expertise, knowledge and huge assets, and decide to trade in. The contract sets out from the start, clearly, what would happen in those circumstances and has no direct effect on your working relationship whilst you are gainfully employed.

For me, the idea of 'protecting' my assets doesn't even come into the equation. I wanted to marry Lisa and she wanted to marry me. Everything I have is now hers, and vice versa. If, and I truly hope it doesn't happen, we were to decide to go our separate ways in years to come, then we would both be entitled to half of the assets because we built the assets up together – it doesn't matter who paid for what or who is working, or who is looking after the kids – as a married couple you are in a partnership and you manage your time, work and finances in ways that both maximize your individual potential and do what is best for the good of the family. Don't marry someone if you are already thinking divorce, divorce, divorce in the back of your mind.

(My wife has just reminded me that it is all very well being sanctimonious when you have no assets really to speak of. What if, for example, there was ten million quid at stake? Which is a fair point ... (imagine that!) Well, I've had a quick think about it and I have decided that I could just about get by on five million. It would be a struggle, but I'd manage.)

A Road Map To Long-lasting Peace

Maybe you don't actually need to physically write out a list, but one of the very early conversations you need to have with your future wife is what you want out of life, your career and your marriage, not just in the short term but until you both retire and beyond. Of course, this plan is going to alter wildly over the coming years, as none of us is a soothsayer, but it is still a very worthwhile exercise and will highlight any dramatic differences in opinion over goals, ambitions and those all-important plans, if any, for kids.

Is your fiancée keen to focus on her career for at least another ten years? Are you planning (if not yearning) to be a stay-at-home dad? Does your fiancée want kids at all, or is she hoping for at least six? Do you know? If not, ask. Mapping out your expectations together for the next

50 years will highlight any major differences in opinion and may expose, before too much damage is done, that your respective plans don't actually seem to involve each other very much over the coming five decades – if that is the case you may well be soon planning how to tell everyone the wedding is off. But that's not even half as bad as having to tell your two kids a few years down the line that Mummy and Daddy don't love each other any more.

Okay, enough of the serious stuff, now there's an engagement party to organize!

Engaging the Enemy

Most people these days have an engagement party. If you do want to celebrate, remember that there will be friends and family members coming to the party that may have never met you before, or, if you've invited them, may not have met your fiancée. So although you may be planning a low-key friendly get-together, one or both of you will be on show. Don't alter your behaviour too much – at the end of the day the two of you have decided to get married for exactly who you are – but equally don't be pulling moonies and challenging ageing uncles to yard-of-ale competitions. Any disapproval, no matter how minor, met at the engagement party has weeks, if not months, to fester. It will then be fed back to either your or your fiancée's parents who will tell you in no uncertain terms what's been said. You could do without that sort of additional pressure and hassle – wedding preparations are already stressful enough.

Call it what you want, but this forthcoming bash is a kind of dress rehearsal for your wedding day. It is therefore almost inevitable that it will cause untold amounts of stress, spiral out of all budgetary control and all end in tears one way or another. Tensions will be high as for the first time many relatives from opposing families will be forced to spend time with one another and make idle chit-chat. There will be big smiles and lots of handshaking, but by the end of the night enemies will have been made and everyone is sure in the knowledge that somewhere down the line the various adversaries are going to have to meet again. And to rub salt in the wound, you're going to have to pay for it all. So with that all in mind, let's open the bubbly and see what happens.

Organizing The Party

The choices for venues are as varied (and can be as costly) as the venue for your wedding reception. There's little point going mad, but equally you're both going to be pretty excited about the news and are likely to want to invite as many friends and members of the family as you can. If you have decided upon a date for the wedding, then be sure to announce that as soon as you can, as friends or relations may have already committed themselves to holidays abroad or even another wedding for the very same weekend as yours. In which case they may wish to treat your engagement party as the wedding itself — including giving you presents!

There is a huge pile of books dedicated to the etiquette of how to invite people to an engagement party — who should send the invites and how they should be written. I apologize to those authors, but what a load of tosh! It's your wedding announcement, not anyone else's, so knock up some invites on the computer, or use a telephone and get partying! If you really want to make a splash I suppose you could be ultra-traditional and place an advert in the Births/Marriages/Deaths section of your local, or even national, newspaper, but, to be honest, the money would be far better spent on the engagement party or the wedding. Update your profile on Friends Reunited if you really want to nark anyone or gloat to others.

Pub, Club Or House Boy?

If all of your guests will fit, then a funky house party is certainly the cheapest option. But most of us are going to need a larger venue and this is where you can be quite clever about negotiations. Many large (nice, trendy) pubs and clubs may waive their hiring fee if:

a: you agree to put some money behind the bar (which you can look at as the hiring fee, whilst also keeping you and your guests very happy), or

b: you can confirm that x number of guests will be coming.

Pubs and clubs make their money on selling booze (and soft drinks, food and snacks) and therefore would rather give you a large expanse of space for free, knowing that you are bringing 80 thirsty and hungry guests, than worrying about 50 quid for a roped-off area in the old snug. Talk to them about it, explain just how much Big Dave will be eating and drinking that night, and they might even throw in a complimentary drink and some canapés for each guest on arrival – if you don't ask, you don't get!

Once you have a venue organized, you really should go to the trouble of finding places where people can stay that are local to the venue. Choose a range of hotels and bed and breakfasts that will suit a range of budgets, ask for discounted rates if guests quote your name and send details in good time, even if it is a simple list of web links sent by email. Obviously, friends who live local to you will hopefully make their way home, but mates from school, university and old work colleagues may be of the mind-set that you are all still 18 at heart, that they've travelled quite far to join you, and now they are completely caned they are wholly intent on coming back to yours after the party to enjoy polishing off the bottles of absinthe and advocat you happen to have left over in the cupboard next to the sink – then promptly falling asleep in a drunken stupor on your new chocolate-brown leather sofa, without taking off their shoes ...

Something For Everyone
The other major concern for the hosts is how well family and friends are going to gel on the night. Some of the family members invited will know you very well (your parents, close cousins, your nan), other family members are being invited because it would be rude not to and it's often easier to sit them in the corner with a pint of mild than it is to face years of derision for leaving them out of the proceedings. But no matter how well your family knows you, they don't know you in quite the same way as your friends do, and that is where catering for such a mixed group is awkward. What you want to achieve is the ideal setup without showing obvious bias for one group in particular, and therefore alienating a significant portion of your guests.

The solution? Well, my brother got engaged recently and had a very cunning plan ... they decided to hire a trendy wine bar for the evening to where everyone was invited. This appealed to the young 'hipsters', and the olds appreciated the fact that there wasn't happy-hardhouse-latino-trance-handbag pumping out of a bass bin, playing havoc with their hearing aids. As midnight approached it was clear that the venue was closing and everyone began to make a move towards the doors. Some tearful exchanges, lots of hugs and it was like Christmas Eve at the taxi rank outside ... However, not terribly well advertised was the fact that there was a pumping club below the bar, and rather slickly Chris had organized complimentary tickets for certain of the guests … so it was like two parties in one. The olds got the chance to wish the couple well and chinwag with the olds from the other side of the family, then they could hop into a cab and get back to the Travelodge just in time for the shipping forecast on Radio 4. Whereas the 'youngsters' got to mingle in the environment in which they felt more comfortable, without fear of being told off by their mum for smoking cigarettes, eating nothing more substantial than two bags of Quavers and a pack of Nobby's Nuts and drinking too many 'alcopop thingies'. It all turned out nice again.

Even with this two-pronged approach to an engagement party, just as you'll find with your actual wedding day, you will not get the chance to speak to anyone for any great length of time – especially your wife-to-be. You will spend the night grinning from ear to ear, wandering around various tables desperately trying to say a word or two to everyone equally. Expect that someone will end up in an argument with someone else, someone will have one too many bitter lemons and someone else will spend the vast majority of the evening crying in the ladies' toilets. All of these fires will need fighting, by you and by the missus, and if you feel exhausted after this event, then bear in mind that it will be at least ten times more intense on your wedding day …

Still want to go ahead? Great. Now there's just the small matter of getting to know your new family … and, of course, there's a wedding to organize!

The In-Laws

Welcome to your
new family, Son

Hello, I'm Your New Mum!

A man goes to see a psychiatrist. He lies on the couch and the psychiatrist asks him what the matter is. The patient replies, 'Yesterday I made a terrible Freudian slip. I was having lunch with my mother-in-law, and I meant to say, "Could you pass the butter?" But I said instead, "You stupid cow, you have completely ruined my life!"' [2]

The mother-in-law has, for many years, been the butt of many a joke. The very mention of her generally raises a groan from any married man. There's a reason for this; for most of us it is a difficult relationship to manage, no matter how hard we try. For instance, we never know, for at least the first ten or so years of marriage, just where it is we stand, precisely, in her eyes. Is it an egotistical thing?

Is it fear? Is it subjugation? After all, the mother-in-law is responsible for bringing into the world the person closest to you, who, in a matter of months is to become your wife. Why this relationship is so charged is probably one of those unanswerable questions that will puzzle the likes of Stephen Hawking for the rest of their and our lives.

There are few worse forms of disapproval known to man than the disapproval of a mother-in-law. (By mother-in-law, I mean, of course, your future wife's mother, not your mum, who is perfect.) In your mother-in-law's eyes you are a disappointment. You just don't measure up. Actually, even if you discovered a cure for cancer and won the Nobel Prize for literature, you still wouldn't measure up. You are just not good enough for her daughter. Sometimes the mother-in-law situation can feel as if some terrible karmic punishment is being meted out upon you for enjoying the carnal pleasures of women, and in particular for deciding to marry one of them. Can all those jokes and stories across nations and cultures be wrong? Can you not now in your mind conjure up the apparition of omnipresent matriarchal despair!!!!! Worse still, is this the spectre of time future: behold the mother-in-law and behold your wife in thirty years' time? Okay boys, time to get a grip. She's your future wife's mother and she's a human being and there is nothing (much) to worry about. You just have to understand what is going on.

You and your mother-in-law have no track record together, no memories of plasters on grazed knees, no extra portions of ice cream because it's Friday night and you've been a good boy. You've never cried in front of this woman (nor would you ever want to) and she's never cried in front of you. She's a sort of half-mum; everything's there, but not quite.

The Cat's Out Of The Bag ...
You may well have been dating your fiancée for many
years, you may have spent a Christmas or two with your
mother-in-law or at least spent a few weekends at her
house and even seen her in her dressing gown and
slippers. But regardless of how long you have known her
as the boyfriend of her daughter, you are now, almost, her
son and that has changed the rules. Now she feels she can
openly comment on your hair, earrings, job, attitude,
grammar, fashion and all the other piss-poor decisions
you've made over the last 30 years. This isn't meant
vindictively, it's just she feels that there's no need for
pretence any more. You're marrying her baby. It's as simple
as that. Your mother-in-law is on overdrive to help her
attain the perfect wedding and no one, not even the
groom, is going to stand in the way. Whether you agree
with this state of things or not, it certainly explains (or will
come to explain) some of the behaviour/comments/snide
remarks/hate mail written in blood that you may receive
over the coming months.

Family And Other Animals
Alfred Radcliffe-Brown, a British social anthropologist who
died in the 1950s, had some interesting ideas about
families and, in particular, about mothers-in-law. Basically
he thought that when a bloke marries into a family he
forms a 'social relationship'. He marries into a family, but
does not actually become part of it. (All married men shout
in unison, 'Too true!') This means there is a sort of strange
'One of us/not one of us' thing going on. (Think Robert De
Niro's character in *Meet the Parents* and the infamous 'circle
of trust' and you'll get my drift.) Although you have lots in
common and many shared interests – daughter/wife,
children/grandchildren, no money/money etc – you also
have big gaps in terms of shared experiences and

expectations, and these can lead to conflict. The upside is that all this is quite normal, and actually helps you to get along whilst also maintaining some distance and preserving your own independent family relations – if you know what I mean.

You are, through the act of marriage, doing two things simultaneously. You are forming your own new family and you are moving into an established family where you must try and find a role ... a suitable place at the table. If you do encounter any 'You're not good enough' stuff from your in-laws, perhaps it is their subconcious way of tempering any possible alpha male conflict, or perhaps it helps maintain a healthy distance between sections of family and promote independence. Who knows what sort of strange human ape stuff is wrapped up in it all?

It's A Tribal Thing

In fact, studies of male Australian aboriginal attitudes to mothers-in-law have come up with some very interesting ideas. How about this? You don't get along with your mother-in-law because, if you did (bearing in mind how many personality traits and, to a lesser extent, looks that your future wife shares with her mother), you might fancy her and want to shag her. (Of course, that's sick and you would be pretty disgusting to even entertain the idea ... although there was a story in the news recently about some Romanian guy who is divorcing his wife to marry his mother-in-law ... but it ain't that common!) Apparently Aborigine blokes not only have some pretty strong taboo stuff going on about touching and being respectful to older women, they have even invented their own avoidance language to deal with mothers-in-law. That's right, they can't even bring themselves to talk about them, so use a specialist terminology when they have to discuss them. Well, maybe that works for them, but in our lives we don't have that option! The mother-in-law is someone you can talk about and talk with.

The main point to remember is that your girlfriend's mother is probably the most important female in her life. She not only gave birth to her, nursed her and helped her grow up, she was possibly instrumental in helping her fashion her identity and ideas, and, let's face it, probably fashioned her ideas about fashion too. From buying starter bras to tampons to discussions about blokes like us, it all comes under her past command. Mother and daughter, we all know how close that can be. Dads and daughters are extremely close too, but in a different way. Sure, dads will warn daughters about blokes, (they are blokes themselves and know what we are like), but the way most blokes deal with daughters is to treat them as their special little girl and spoil them rotten right up until the time you march down the aisle, and possibly beyond. So her mum is really, really important in her life and will continue to remain so, whether you like it or not and especially if you intend to have kids.

The Last Taboo

Even if her mother drives your fiancée mad and she complains about her endlessly. Even if her mother can send her into fits of temper and introspection that surprise even you, don't think her mother is open season for criticism. If you constantly criticize her mother or start banging on about her like an enraged madman, you are going to really upset your future wife. Here's the rub: her mother can criticize you, but you must really, really limit your criticism of her. The payback, though, is that even if your mother-in-law actually does hate you (which she probably does not, and is merely trying to establish rules and find ways of working together) ... even if she thinks that you are an immature, football-obsessed example of lumpen, proletarian, Cockney filth, she has to get on with you too. You are marrying her daughter and you may be the future father of her grandchildren and, most importantly, you are her daughter's choice. That leaves you wiggle room, even if that room happens to be the size of a discarded box of Swan Vestas matches.

Try To Forget The Clichés

In fact, many men get on very well with their mother-in-law. They have an adult and close relationship together, one that is often very supportive. If there are difficulties, then you have to remember that you are entering new relationships and, in the same way as you wouldn't expect to make friends and be really popular on the very day you just started a new job, why should you expect to fit in straight away with a new group of people who also happen to be part of your family? Just remember how complex your own family relations can be and then cast your eye over your new relatives. Moreover, the mother-in-law is often the butt of jokes as she is a relatively safe target. Start taking the proverbial out of your wife for being a terrible cook and the net result is you are not going to get laid. Start taking the proverbial out of her dad and there may be a fight – so the mother-in-law is someone who is both safe ground and a cultural stereotype. Men love to present themselves as hard done by and oppressed, and the wife's mother can be just perfect for that.

Do Try To Get Along

The golden rule in any given situation is to try to get along with your in-laws. If you are at work and there is someone in the office whom you need to cooperate with, but who always makes your life difficult, you don't take them out to the car park and give them a pasting, do you? You develop a strategy for working with them. That's what you have to do here – get along and hope things get better. In many cases, not surprisingly, difficulties with in-laws and mothers-in-law often ease over time. When they start to see you in a more positive light, perhaps because of your job or when you become a father, or simply as you get older and more mature, then you will gain greater acceptance. There will still be fights but that's life. Here are some guidelines of things not to do:

a. Never rant and rage about her parents – even if your future wife does

b. Never criticize your wife in front of her mother (or father) – they don't like you that much as it is!

c. Do not expect to fit in with her family straight away – you are marrying the daughter, not her mum and dad.

d. Do develop a long-term strategy. Try your best to make your relationship with your in-laws work. Draw on all your reserves of patience and understanding and learn to control your temper.

e. However, also stand up for yourself and stick to your guns – you are going to be the head/joint partner of your own family; maintain your independence.

There is also the baptism of fire that is the wedding preparations to bear in mind. These will invariably be a major focus for you and your mother-in-law right about now. This 'distraction' will no doubt cloud and override the focus of this new, blossoming relationship between you both ... sorry, mate.

Call Me Dad ...

In theory, your relationship with your father-in-law should be a little more clear-cut. There aren't many father-in-law jokes in existence and the fact that you are both blokes should make communication if not easy, at least straightforward. In fact, throughout history there are many examples of fathers-in-law and their sons-in-law getting on fabulously; forming great companies, business partnerships and dynasties. It would appear that the only real barrier between you and your father-in-law getting along well is the difference in age and outlook. Mind you, most of us work with blokes who are older than us and who may also be our mates, so that should be a relatively minor hurdle. I'm sure there are even cases of dads and boyfriends remaining friends long after the girlfriend has moved on to new pastures. But for many of the respondents to my questionnaire, it seems that the real world is very different from the theory.

One guy, a consultant doctor and an Oxbridge graduate no less, actually caught his father-in-law telling guests at his wedding that he considered his daughter's choice to be motivated by her wanting to climb the social ladder and that he was sorry his daughter felt she needed to jump up a class. Needless to say, relations have not been good since. In another story, I learnt that a future father-in-law told the poor bloke asking for his daughter's hand that he would not be able to keep his daughter in the lifestyle she expected and deserved and that if they proceeded to get married they could expect no help or comfort from his quarter. Many blokes will report cordial but not great relationships with their father-in-law. In fact, it would appear that many fathers-in-law are singularly disinterested in their new 'son'. In my own personal circumstances, I hasten to add, I have been treated as one of the family from day one. In fact, rather worryingly, over the past couple of years I've got even lazier with a razor than ever before, and now I have even started to look like Bill. How weird is that!

Show Some Respect, Son!
The fact of the matter is that for the father-in-law, having to deal with a permanent new male member of the family, or at least a half-member of the family, is a bit awkward. Step into his shoes for a minute. Your daughter has had boyfriends in the past, some of whom she may have been very keen on and some of whom may have treated her very badly. His daughter is one of the most important and cherished people in his life and he wants her to be happy and to enjoy her life. He has been worried about her and cared for her since she was a baby and the depth of his love and experiences with her will be enormous. Then you turn up, out of the blue (or out of the pub) with your swagger and your cheeky grin and no remorse about sitting in his favourite chair.

He doesn't know you from Adam and you're supposed to try to get along. He may instinctively like you, but initially he is not going to be too friendly with you as you may be only a temporary fixture. Plus, he will hear about all of your temporary break-ups and arguments and he will have had to listen to both his daughter's and his wife's commentary about you. He may also have seen you out socially and know (and have an opinion about) your job prospects and personal finance. To begin with he will probably reserve judgement, even if he has a pretty good idea of what you are like. However, once you decide to get engaged, his opinion of you will begin to firm up.

The Father/Daughter Relationship

Remember, too, that your relationship with your father-in-law will depend on how well his daughter gets on with him. They may not be close. He may have simply not been there for her. He may just be a very different kind of person from you. The idea that all women marry a surrogate for their own father is not necessarily true. Her father may well have been a male role model, but not necessarily the exact male role model that she wants to marry. She may have chosen you precisely because you possess different qualities to her father.

Another possibility to consider is that *you* may not actually like *him* very much. Indeed, you may not like the way he talks to you or the way he treats your future wife. The rule here, again, is to keep it to yourself. For a start, relations between you may get better over time.

Whatever happens, you are likely to be tied together for a long time. If you have a stand-up row with him and call him an absolute idiot you are going to burn your bridges. Even if a father-in-law actively dislikes you, he may still help you for the sake of his daughter. There is no law that you should get on with him. There is no reason why he should like you or you should like him, and there is almost certainly going to be an element of competition between you. So you will have to deal with the occasional back-handed compliment and the odd dig about how crap you are at DIY repairs, even if he thinks the world of you. Don't be all 'He doesn't like me ... sob, sob!'

As I said earlier, the general rule, for everybody's sake, is to try to get along. Although for all sorts of reasons it does tend to be easier to get along with the father-in-law than the mother-in-law, whatever the circumstances, you have to try to develop a working relationship. You may not have to get along with your bride's sister or her mates, but you really must try to get along with her mum and dad.

Anyway, come on, mate, you probably already have some idea of how your future in-laws feel about you. If it's good, well, try not to blot your copybook during all the stresses and strains of the wedding planning. If it isn't, then develop some plans to manage the relationship rather than creating conflict. Be diplomatic and polite in decision making – even if that means jumping up and down with anger in the privacy of your own home. You can limit the times and places you meet and, you never know, sometimes even bad relationships get better – say, if you get her dad's car fixed cheaply, or give them a grandson or get a promotion at work ... or win the lottery ... which brings us neatly on to the next chapter.

The Pay-Out

Cash, cars and getting
your financial house
in order

Weddings, no matter how small, cost money. In fact, they cost so much money that you need to get your financial house in order immediately. The more organized you are, right from the moment you get engaged, the more confident you can be that the wedding, and the marriage that you are entering into, will be a huge success − financially, as well as every other way. None of us likes thinking about money matters too much − they are boring and time-consuming. Plus we know that any 'investigation' into the way we manage our finances will expose just how much money we waste every month on non-essential items − booze, fags, meals out, PlayStation® games, CDs ... The truth will probably hurt but you'll be better off facing it than continuing to bury your head in the sand.

Joined By The Sort Code

You may, of course, be a long-established couple who have shared a bank account for absolutely ages – if so, that's even more reason to read on. Whether you're both new to sharing your finances or whether it's old hat, you are going to need a new bank account set up specifically to help you manage the wedding. This shouldn't cost you anything; just have a word with one of your existing banks and fill in the forms. You'll want a current account because although you will miss out on the miniscule interest rates offered for savings accounts, you will want to have access to your funds 24 hours a day, along with a debit card, a cheque book and possibly, as the big day looms, an overdraft …

Once the wedding is over, the account won't go to waste; change its status to a savings account and you can use it to save up for home improvements, holidays abroad, or … pitter patter, pitter patter, what's that we hear?

The moment the account is activated you need to start paying money in, because very soon you are going to be paying money out, in fact an awful lot. Your first job is to pay in any large amounts of cash that just happen to be hanging around awaiting their opportunity to help you out – you know, the five grand under the floorboards you were saving for a rainy day, or the seven thousand you set up in the tracker fund you organized on your eighteenth birthday, specifically for your wedding day … it's not there any more, you say? Oh dear. Well, like the rest of us you are going to have to organize a monthly payment from your main bank account(s). Be sure to make the direct debit payment the day after you are paid your salary, so it isn't squandered on that must-have DVD. The amount you set aside (multiplied by the number of months until the wedding) will be the bedrock of your wedding funds. Shocking, isn't it?

Ask The Family

So, where's the rest of it going to come from? Well, ideally you'll be able to speak with your respective families about what, if any, assistance they can provide. Hopefully the parents will agree between themselves to pay for x, y and maybe even z – if so, get the prices, confirm your chosen supplier and get the cash off Pops and Pops-to-be without further ado. Insist on making the wedding account the single point of entry and exit for all monies relating to the wedding, otherwise it gets very messy.

Dad, Don't Suppose There's Any Chance Of...?

It's not easy to ask your own parents, let alone your in-laws, for cash – you and your fiancée probably both flew the nest over a decade ago and you like to think that you're both independent, self-supporting, mature taxpayers who have got over the 'Can I have a tenner to go to the pub?' sort of stage. And you have. It's just that a wedding is a once-in-a-lifetime (hopefully!) experience and many parents with even only a hundred pounds to spare will gladly donate it (as well as their time, experience, views and opinions) to see their son or daughter married. Don't forget that seeing your offspring get married is a major rite of passage for parents and therefore you might not find that they need much encouragement to help at all. In fact, they do know that you're independent and all the rest of it, and respect that, so all they're waiting for is the green light from you that a bit of cold hard cash, right now, would be terribly useful!

Do not make it, or let it become, a competitive race between the parents over who is paying for what, and how much or little the other party is paying – any help is welcome. You need to be the one making sure everyone keeps it in perspective. Let them have their one 'tangible contribution', i.e. parents A paid for the dress and parents

B paid for the honeymoon (you wish!), but any other cash just got paid into the pot and helped pay for everything else.

You don't want to labour the point or unsettle either set of parents, but you won't be out of order to start hinting at a financial contribution the same week that you announce your intention to be wed – the longer everyone has to get used to the news, the longer they have to sort things out, and, hopefully, the more assistance you will receive.

The Cost Of Money

There is a 'cost' to receiving cash from the in-laws for your wedding. They want payback, and often not in a financial sense, but in an influence sense. If they've given you x amount of cash towards the cost of the catering, then you can rest assured that whatever meal you would like to have on the day, unless it happens to be their decision too, you're unlikely to get it. This isn't a deliberate snipe at your culinary tastes, it's just a gentle reminder that the cash offered to you came with shareholder privileges and voting rights, and, as majority stakeholders, your in-laws are taking this opportunity to remind you that their uncle Albert (whom you've never met) is now invited to the wedding and can't be within fifty metres of red meat, which means you're all having chicken.

In fact, long after the wedding cake has been consumed and you and your wife are beginning to show the signs of ageing, that generous financial help you received at the time of your wedding will continue to be in the air – maybe not mentioned by name, but alluded to, with phrases like 'We've supported you financially in the past' or 'We were behind you in the early days.' When this is mentioned, then something is required in return. Now, most of the time it will probably just be a lift to Tesco for some milk, but even if you have paid back the money, in full, and with interest, you will still be indebted for life, and don't forget it, *Son*.

So if that seems like too high a price to pay, and if you can get away with taking a loan out for the missing funds, it might be best to take it, no matter what the interest rates, because it may well hurt far less than a lifetime of guilt!

Ask The Bank

You may have to consider taking out a loan to cover all or part of the costs of the wedding. Bear in mind that the repayments will begin the month after you get the money, so if you can only afford to pay £100 into the wedding fund each month at the moment, how on earth do you plan to pay the further £100 extra a month, if you were to borrow £5,000? It is only through working over your finances and clarifying what help you can expect from family members that you can swiftly come to the conclusion that the castle wedding in Scotland with helicopter taxis for all the guests was a great idea ... but not really a viable option.

Extras Are Just That ...

At all times during this rather depressing business of talking about money, remember that primarily you are getting married because you love each other (in richness and in poorness) and family and friends wouldn't dream of judging you if your wedding reception is not a blatant display of opulent decadence. They are the people who love you and, at the end of the day, they would be over the moon for you even if you dressed in sack cloth, made them all buy their own chippy dinner and shared a bottle of wine between the lot of you. And also remember that providing anything more than the above is your choice, and your choice only. Spend the money on a fancy wedding only if you can and you want to. It's not a time for one-upmanship or about keeping up appearances – it's about you two beginning a new life together. Do not financially cripple yourself over an ice sculpture and some fancy hors d'oeuvres!

Facing Reality

Through your own rough sums, the early promises of financial assistance from family and some investigations into the possibility of either applying for a loan or taking equity out of your home, you will be beginning to paint a none-too-pretty picture of the amount the two of you have to play with in terms of your wedding. Whatever amount you have raised will never feel like enough to satisfy your dearest wishes. So the earlier you are both able to come to terms with how much you are going to need to compromise, the better. Then the rest of the wedding plans should be plain sailing – well, not quite, but you'll be far better equipped to deal with disappointment.

How Much Did You Say?

So, you've saved, begged and borrowed money and now you've come up with a figure to spend on your wedding. You make a few calls and it quickly becomes very evident that weddings are expensive. Really, really expensive. You've earmarked a couple of hundred for photography and the cheapest quotes are over five hundred. The same for flowers, catering, room hire … Why? Well, at first it might appear a bit of a chicken-and-egg scenario – are weddings expensive because the services you require are expensive and it all just adds up, or, are they expensive because the providers know you are arranging a marriage, and will stump up the cash somehow? I think it's the latter – everyone's out to make money and what better way than to cash in on other people's happiness? Adding an extra 20 per cent isn't going to deter the bride if that's what she wants for her wedding day: 'Damn it, no one and no amount is going to get in the way of my special day.' Neither you nor your fiancée are going to want to cut any corners and you're going to want the best you can afford; and, on top of that, you will be convinced to raise the bar even higher through very devious up-selling techniques every time. And therein lies the problem. Everyone involved in providing services for weddings knows the rules, and the rules are that getting a wedding job is a licence to print your own cash. Heartless bastards.

Post-wedding Blues
Throwing every penny you can possibly beg, borrow and steal at a wedding will almost certainly guarantee that you have a party to remember ... but that's going to do you no long-term favours if you manage to financially cripple yourselves in the process. A wedding should be fun. It can be lavish in parts and you will want to be gracious hosts, but no guest is going to criticize your efforts on their behalf, so keep everything in perspective. One of the most cited reasons for divorce is arguments over money and how money is managed – don't be getting into bad habits before there's even a ring on her finger!

Buying A Home

Maybe you and your wife-to-be own a house/flat together, maybe you own a home each, or maybe you are both renting separately or together – whatever the circumstances, you are about to live as man and wife, in a bed together, and in a home together, legally, in both the eyes of your God(s) and the eyes of the law (not to mention the eyes of the Inland Revenue and your local council, which often has more serious implications...). This often means that a decision needs to be made about where you are going to live. And how is it all going to work out financially?

What's Mine Is Yours
Married life is no longer as cut and dried as 'You pay for this and I pay for that.' Your finances will become one – often with an 'unfair' focus on *your* bank account. But that's part of the deal – what's hers is yours and vice versa. You may actually feel like you are taking a step backwards – especially if prior to married life you both shared the mortgage and once you are married the mortgage will solely become your responsibility ... Get over it. What does it matter which bank account the cost of this or that comes out of? You're married now and that means sharing. You must (because she certainly will) look upon your joint incomes as your *joint* income. The funds may come from a variety of sources, but they are yours (plural) to spend how you (plural) see fit. Yes, you might now be expected to pay the entire mortgage repayment instead of half, but think how much of your partner's salary that frees up to spend on the two of you going out and enjoying life as a married couple – so, she picks up the tab in the restaurant more often than feels comfortable to your sensitive male ego; but it is *your* (plural) home, which you are paying for, that you will both return to this evening after the waiter has (apparently) scoffed at the sight of a woman paying for a meal. Get over it, you Neanderthal!

If you are renting, then the early years of marriage should be the time that you begin at least to consider the prospect of owning your own home (albeit with the essential aid of a mortgage). Rent, quite simply, is a great musical but a terrible waste of money. It is dead money: instant profit for the landlord that is doing you no favours at all. The sooner you can, you both need to start looking for a mortgage and owning your own home, even if all you can afford is a one-bedroom flat in the dodgiest area in the world. Take it. You'll be on the ladder and earning money on house prices instead of simply feeding someone else's pockets. This simple act of buying a home is actually you taking a huge step to securing your mutual financial future and security. It can feel like an impossible mountain to climb and for most of us it is pretty crippling, but like the Corkscrew at Alton Towers, once you're on, you're on. There's no getting off until the ride has come to a complete stop and the safety barriers are removed – chances are you're going to make a handsome profit in the meantime and the next time you see Carol Vorderman on the telly offering loans to 'homeowners', you'll be able to smile smugly to yourself knowing you qualify and deciding whether or not you want to phone that number.

Marriage, you are quickly beginning to realize, is all about compromise and commitment, and I don't think there are many things more profound than entering into a debt arrangement of over £150,000 to tie the two of you together. Thinking about it rationally, what is it about a wedding speech that possibly warrants giving us sleepless nights when the thought of signing a mortgage agreement should really leave us quaking in our shoes and banging our head against a wall with the sheer insanity of it!

Dirty Old Town?

Where you will live as a married couple might be a no-brainer or it can be an unspoken, moot point. Whatever the circumstances in which you met – be it an introduction at work, through friends, through the Internet or just two lonely souls that happened to be at the same place, at the same time, one evening in a nightclub – you met in a certain place where you may or may not already live and now you're planning on getting married. Where exactly is your marital home going to be? What about in five years? Are you likely to be sent around the country because of work commitments? Do you live where you live because that's where you were brought up? Would you like to continue to live near your family because you are intending to have children and some 'on tap' babysitting would prove very useful?

All these questions need to be answered, sooner rather than later. Location is important, but our rationale changes as the years pass – an ideal location for ensuring the best job opportunities may or may not be the ideal place to bring up a young family. Do you have a parking space outside your home or do you have to park where you can and walk half a mile every evening? You won't be able or willing to do that with a toddler in your arms.

If you are at the point where you are ready to buy a home, now is an ideal opportunity to choose a suitable location for your new 'family' lifestyle, and that might not be in the area where you currently live ...

Wills

Continuing on the sober, grown-up theme, I'm sorry to be so tedious but it is of paramount importance that you and your partner make a will if you haven't done so already. Organize a will immediately. Wills are reasonably straightforward and not too expensive (certainly in comparison to the potential legal fees that either you or your partner may incur if you have to sort it out after a death).

All a will is really saying is that you want certain items of property or other investments to go to specific people when you die. Just as you control the distribution of your wealth (estate) when you are alive, these are your instructions after your death.

Dying without a will means that the state wins, and it will be a hard battle for your family to win back what should rightfully be theirs, without at least paying a penalty. Contact your solicitors, or find a solicitor in your local area if you don't have one. If you have any children in the future, then be sure to revisit the will to include him or her – assuming you would like your child to benefit!

How Much Are You Worth ... Dead?
Right about now, you're probably feeling young, fit and healthy. You have a beautiful fiancée and life is looking pretty sweet. And it is. But it won't always be the case. You need to think long-term about your health and all the dangers there are lurking out there on the roads or in the air. Many things might cause you or your future wife to die. As grim a topic as it is, there's no getting away from the fact that you and I are mortal. We will all die; I just hope it's later rather than sooner.

Your death is obviously going to disrupt you, but not half as much as it's going to disrupt those you leave behind. Planning for their financial future is essential, and organizing some life assurance now is absolutely critical. If you're a homeowner, then the chances are you already have a policy in place – check to see who the beneficiary is. How much are you assured for? If it's just the value of the house, then that's something, but some extra cash to at least pay for your funeral might be an idea, if not a lump sum of cash to help the transition period of adjustment after you're gone. You may or may not have kids at the moment; what about them? They could do with a little something to help them get started in life, further down the line. Have a think, talk this through with your fiancée – you're probably thinking that the last thing you want right now is additional monthly expenditure; you're in the middle of saving for a wedding! But that's no excuse because there's a chance (albeit incredibly, infinitesimally small) that you won't make it to the wedding ...

When You're Old And Wrinkly
You know what's coming, don't you? Pensions. Other than mortgages, probably the most boring, convoluted, deliberately confusing product offered by the financial services industry. If you've got one set up yourself, or you contribute to a pension scheme through work, great. If you haven't, sort it out. You're not getting any younger and the money you save now will be worth so much more than the money you pay in as you approach retirement age. It's frightening. Yes, you've got the wedding to worry about, but you'll also, very soon, have a wife to think about and that means both of you knowing what will happen to you in the long term and how you are going to make ends meet until the life assurance mentioned above kicks in ...

Got A New Motor?
'A car, I'm not going to buy a new car now...' You're right, now would be a very silly time to splash out on a new car, but what if the car you currently drive was originally bought with the carefree couple in mind? What if you've decided that children are going to be on the horizon very soon? What if selling your car and trading it in for something far more suitable for a family with small children would actually free up some cash towards the wedding, and set you up ready for carting a newborn baby around? Think about it. I know family wagons don't have the same appeal as sporty little two-seater roadsters, but you're a

married man now. This is what happens when you're married, you have to make sensible decisions ... you're not long away from a cardigan, slippers and a pipe.

Debt Mountain

Most of us have been guilty at some stage in our past of running a bit riot with the various forms of credit so easily available. I was no exception. Student loans, bank loans, credit cards, a severe lack of savings all added up to make my personal balance sheet a dream for the lenders but pretty miserable for me. As we had a baby before we got married, it was the prospect of becoming a dad that became the catalyst for me doing something about it – I opted for a consolidation loan and eventually cleared the debt. Now you are on the verge of getting married, it might be the time to sort out your debts into one clear monthly payment and the lowest rate of interest that you can find. The consolidation loan could be arranged so that there is some excess left over that can be put towards the wedding. Try and get some advice from an independent financial adviser and see what they can recommend in your situation.

Avoiding Financial Meltdown

For the next few months, every penny is really going to count. No one is suggesting that you should become social hermits or eat beans on toast every day for the remaining months before your wedding, but there is little point moaning about the wedding being too expensive or finding it difficult to know where the money is going to come from to pay the DJ, when you continue to go out with your mates to the pub a couple of times a week. It might only be 'a couple of pints' but 20 quid every session will soon eat away at your spare cash and this would be better kept in the 'wedding' bank account to cover all of the expenses you already know about, and those you are still to learn about. Don't alienate your friends, just suggest a few tins round at the house, rather than going out to the pub – you'll *all* save on the ancillary spending as well: the fruit machine, the bar snacks, the pool table, the taxi and the kebab ...

If your fiancée is a bit of a shopping fan, you wouldn't be out of order to suggest that the Jimmy Choo spending sprees could wait until after the wedding (unless, of course, the shoes are actually *for* the wedding). There should certainly be a spending freeze on home furnishings and trips to Ikea – you're about to get married, for goodness' sake: just think how many bits and bobs you're going to acquire; all you have to do is wait a couple of months and let someone else pay.

Look After The Pennies ...
If you're the sort of bloke who likes to grab a sandwich, drink and bag of crisps at lunchtime, stop. Immediately. That's about £5 a day you are needlessly spending. Make the extra effort and buy in some nice rolls from the supermarket, freeze them, and then get up ten minutes earlier and make your own butties! Five pounds a day, five times a week will save you about £100 a month (even after you've bought your sandwich materials!). If your wedding's a year away you'll have over an extra grand to play with!

No more multimedia – no computer games, no DVDs (no matter how good an offer, or how attractive the lead actress), no CDs, no more paid-for Internet downloads. Make do with what you've got for the remaining time before the wedding. It's not that hard, and think, by the time the wedding's over, you'll have changed your mind about buying most titles, or will have had the chance to see them round at a mate's house, and if you're still determined to purchase, you'll find everything's now in platinum edition or on special offer and you'll only pay a fraction of the original price.

The same is true for holidays abroad or even weekends away – your honeymoon is just around the corner ... It will be the greatest trip of your life thus far. Is a weekend away in a Holiday Inn really necessary; do you really both need to go off to Spain on a cheap flight, just for the sake of it? No, you don't. Save the money and you'll be able to ensure that your honeymoon is truly luxurious.

It's going to hurt (probably you more than her) but you need to tone down your television expenditure – it's hard, but you're going to have to get rid of the extra channels on your cable or satellite deal. By all means keep the basic package but shave off the movie channels, the sports channels (the porn...). You don't need them, at least not until after the wedding. It could be a saving of over £20 a month. Add that to your 'less time in the pub' resolution and your new home-made sandwich regime and you're beginning to talk about significant amounts of cash to play with. Conservatively, there could be over two grand extra in the bank account in the next 12 months – which is going to be a serious help.

Show Me The Money

I'm not sure if it is ethical or not, but it's a dog-eat-dog world and I would personally use any tactics available to help the marriage cause. Marriage is seen as a stepping stone, a rite of passage that turns the 'lad', no matter how old, into the 'man'. It's up there with fatherhood in terms of making people consciously or unconsciously treat you differently and therefore it would be a wise move indeed to inform your boss at your earliest convenience – you're not looking for congratulations or a pat on the back (well, not in the literal sense) but what you are looking for is recognition of this life-changing event. That recognition may come in a change of circumstances at work, over the coming months.

A canny boss will realize that a male employee who is about to get married is unlikely to be looking for work elsewhere. If your boss likes you, then this will be a welcome relief. However, the canny boss will also recognize that (however incorrectly) there is a chance the marriage will be quickly followed by a baby, and that's when cogs begin to turn, hopefully to your benefit. A new baby will mean added cost, so you're probably going to be looking for more money, or you'll have to move on. If you're good at your job, then he's going to want to keep hold of you ... and here he is now ... knock, knock ... 'Can we have a chat about your salary...?'

Every Little Helps

The asking for money shouldn't really stop with parents; in fact, you could involve siblings and extended family in the equation by requesting cash up front instead of wedding presents. You may not feel you know your uncles and cousins well enough to ask the question without it feeling awkward – well, that's what your parents are for. They'll ask on your behalf via their siblings to avoid any embarrassments. It could be that a couple of uncles, aunties and cousins club together and suddenly the catering bill is halved or completely taken care of. Suddenly this wedding lark is looking a bit more manageable and your family can feel they have truly contributed personally rather than spending an afternoon in John Lewis buying a present they know you want, but feeling like no thought went into the gift. At the end of the day I'm sure you'd much prefer to have no overdraft than five kettles!

I Want That One. And That, And That ...

Speaking of which, for many couples a wedding can be like the ultimate Christmas come early – presents, thousands of them! Yes, a big part of the wedding process is the receiving of gifts. If you've been living together for years, or even if you've been living alone for any period of time, then, chances are, you already have all the bits and bobs you truly need for married life – the washing machine, the iron, the kettle, the novelty slippers ... but that doesn't mean we don't want more and it certainly doesn't mean that guests will make that assumption and not buy you a gift.

The jury's still out with most of us over whether the act of creating and drawing people's attention to a wedding list is somewhat presumptuous and rude, but common sense will tell you that everyone coming will want to buy you a present and would prefer to buy you something that you need and want. Therefore, giving people a list of exactly what you want is the ideal solution. And it is – but that doesn't stop the whole process feeling a bit weird.

Most large stores now offer a wedding list service. This can range from a personal shopper assigned to you (you will have to book an appointment, not just show up and flick your fingers, unless one of you is famous) who will personally give you a tour of the shop and note down each of your wishes, or you can simply browse catalogues and note down some code numbers and prices. Or you can post your wedding list online via e-tailers such as Amazon. Whichever method the store employs, it all pretty much boils down to the same thing – you make a list of everything you want, being sure to appeal to every price range, and guests can order the stuff and have it delivered either to your home or to the actual wedding venue. Have your presents delivered to your home, it is much safer, but try not to open them before you are married! Be sure to store wrapped presents out of sight, otherwise you are asking for a break-in.

Whilst there should be lots of stuff at the entry price range, don't feel bad about putting more expensive items on the list – firstly, there might actually guests out there happy to pay the extra, or more likely there might be a group of friends that would rather club together and buy you something big. If you don't ask, you don't get. However, an old work colleague/friend of mine recently posted his *two* wedding lists online so that the transatlantic guests could buy from the wedding list based nearest to them – unfortunately, the particular stores they'd decided upon were a little bit on the pricy side and the cheapest item available was over £100, for a towel … Now, I'm no cheapskate, but £100 for a towel? I'm sorry, but he got something completely different and it didn't cost a quarter of that. There's making the life of your guests easier and, quite frankly, there's taking the proverbial. Put lots of mid-price items on there. Most people will be looking to spend between £30 and £50.

Flowers In Her Hair …

I don't know about you, but for me flowers are flowers. I even worked for a company selling the things on the Internet for a while, so probably know a bit more about the cut-flower market than the average bloke – however, I just can't get that excited or interested in them. They're all nice, in fact they're all really pretty, but I'm just not fussed. What bothers me, really, is that the moment the things are hacked out the ground, they're dying and in about one week (if you're lucky sometimes) the things will be going in the bin. And, they're so bloody expensive. Bah, humbug.

Flowers, of course, are part and parcel of the whole wedding thang and of course we arranged for a bridal bouquet, buttonholes and corsages for all concerned. They looked lovely. The choice of what flowers will be worn, or carried, by whom is something that your fiancée or certainly one of her entourage will gladly take the lead on; so sit back and relax and keep working on that speech.

Something to bear in mind, and I'm sure your chosen florist will let you know specifics, is that cut flowers are seasonal, just like fruit and vegetables – when stuff's in season it's obviously cheaper than when it's not. However, the floral industry is big business and to keep up with our 24/7 demanding needs, there are acres of flowers being grown under glass (hothouses) in the UK and across Europe – so certain flowers, such as roses, won't be growing naturally in Kenya right now, but you can bet there's a flower farm in Holland that's about to crop … and if the girl wants pew decorations cascading with birds of paradise, then, by God, she'll get them. But if she also likes orchids and alstroemeria just as much, then, with a bit of persuasion, you might get three times the amount of flower for your cash. Her favourite flower, after all, can always be included in the display for the top table, or if suitable, within the bridal bouquet, and your favourite flower could always make an appearance in your buttonhole – you big pansy.

Shop around for florists, demand to see a wedding portfolio, and better yet if you can get a recommendation from a friend who was happy with the service they got, use them. Floral arranging is an art and there are some highly trained practitioners out there; it's also an easy business to set up with no formal training – so do your homework, otherwise your bride may be walking down the aisle with what appears to be a 'bouquet' you nabbed from a Shell forecourt coming home drunk in the early hours of the morning. Again.

A Floral Problem Shared Is A Floral Problem Halved

You are bound to come across several hitches in your quest to get hitched, and one of them might be that you may not be the only couple who have arranged to get married in that particular church or venue on that particular day. If this is so, the worst that can happen is that there's a bit of extra traffic (both cars and pedestrians) around the entrance of the church as one wedding party leaves and another arrives. On the positive side, if there are two weddings taking place, then there's the possibility that you can save a bit of cash by asking the priest/pastor/vicar/minister/holy man or woman for contact details for the other couple, and between you the four of you could organize the church flowers. Obviously you'll have to agree on colours, style and most importantly price, but you'll immediately shave a couple of hundred quid off your total bill which could be better spent elsewhere, without, hopefully compromising your (fiancée's) wishes. Bear in mind that the second wedding (or more accurately, the guests of the second wedding) will also benefit from actually taking the flowers away with them.

Using Protection

Believe it or not, it is now possible to take out wedding

insurance. (Given that certain celebrities have insured their hands, feet and backsides, maybe it's not that odd after all.) Sadly, it won't pay out if your bride gets itchy feet and decides not to arrive at the church, but it will provide financial relief if you've paid, for example, 75 per cent of the catering bill upfront and the company goes out of business before you get to taste the leek-and-stilton soup starter. Yes, it's an additional expense and not a cheap one, but to put in into perspective, the average wedding now costs about £12,000. That's comparable to the price of a decent car and you wouldn't dream of spending that much on a car and not having it insured ... The other argument is that if you sit down for a second and work out the number of suppliers involved in any one wedding (the caterers, hotels, florist, bar, dressmakers/hirers, travel agent, car hire, church and so on), the chances of something untoward happening to one of these organizations within the next nine or so months is actually a real possibility. As a betting man you might decide to take your chances, but then again, as a betting man how many times have you backed the winner of the Grand National?

A Quote For This, A Quote For That
Even if you've both got a mapped-out version of the wedding in your heads – and you are both definitely thinking about the *same* wedding – be sure to get a couple of alternative quotes for each service that you require. In essence, try and get an economy, mid-range and luxury price for everything. During the early months you will both be so full of excitement and verve about the wedding that those soon-to-be-tedious phone calls explaining your every wish and desire (not to forget that it's yet another excuse to tell someone that you are getting married) will be an absolute pleasure to make. Then as the weeks and months pass and you come round to making very important

decisions about the actual wedding, you will have all of the ammunition and information required to make informed decisions, quickly. If you've gone two grand over budget on the dress then something will have to give, and referring to your overflowing 'wedding folder' will provide the answer, and you won't have to go back to basics, and start making introductory phone calls this late on in the day.

Modern Love

One way you could really save on costs is by sending out all invitations and so forth by email. But if even you can't face being that much of a cheapskate, then there are many other ways computers and the Internet can help in your wedding preparations. If it's your kind of thing, then it really is worth setting up your own wedding site. Computers may have already helped you immensely with your wedding preparations (financial spreadsheets, researching supplier websites, wedding invitation designs and so on). The next step is to create a wedding website; if you're a dab hand with HTML, then it might be something you can knock up yourself. For the rest of us there are numerous web-based template sites you can easily adapt to suit your needs. (Just type *+Wedding +Websites* into Google and take a look – many companies are now offering a free trial, so that you can see if you're happy with the look and feel before you commit to buying.)

Don't feel you have to get an all-singing, all-dancing website up and running on day one – it's an organic process and you can add a bit here and there as you get the chance. If you decide on a web-based application (which means you log on to your site, via the Internet, and edit directly onto the page) then it's a great way to waste an hour or two at work – but I'm sure you're far too diligent and conscientious to even consider that!

Just as you had someone look over your wedding invitations before they went to print, be sure to have someone check any new text that is going to be posted on the website – silly mistakes won't paint the author in the best light.

Don't worry, it's not pretentious to have your own website – bear in mind people have websites for their cat! This is your wedding, which is as good an excuse as any to get on to the World Wide Web and advertise your love for your partner. This can be a great project for you to get into while your fiancée concentrates on all those other things that seem to be taking up all her time recently.

Why The Web?
Well, for a start you probably got sick, very quickly, of telling everyone the exact details of the engagement – why not write the experience up as a story and post it online – send everyone you know the web address and save a fortune on phone calls. Friends and family, especially if they live some distance from you, will be keen to follow the progress of your wedding preparations and to learn a bit more about the bride/groom. Your site is the ideal place to show the details of the wedding. (Don't worry, it won't mean there will be tonnes of gatecrashers looking for free booze, because only your nearest and dearest will know the URL (web address). You could password-protect entry if you're really paranoid!)

Most importantly, you can include links through to the local hotels and guesthouses to allow your guests to book their accommodation online – it is your responsibility to make sure that the link points to the right destination, otherwise you'll be getting married in Southampton and your guests will all be booked into the Marriot in Aberdeen! Last but not least, your wedding website is the ideal place to offer links through to your wedding list, so that guests can buy exactly what you want online, which most people are very comfortable doing nowadays.

As an example of how a website can help unite transatlantic guests, one of my friends created a site for his wedding a while back, which is still hosted at the address in the Useful Contacts.

Pic Me

A website is always far more exciting if it's chock-full of images – pictures of the two of you, pictures of where you live, any family pets, children and any sneak peeks of the church and reception venue. What did you look like as children? Or as teenagers? Are there any photos of the two of you together from the very early days of your relationship? If you are fond of any particular sports or charities, you can include links through to the relevant websites on your site. If you're trying to raise money for the wedding by selling things through eBay, put a link on your site through to your current auctions – capitalize on a very captive audience!

Getting A Bit Technical

If you really get into the whole website business, you will want to optimize your images for the web – and this means using graphic software to alter the resolution/dpi (dots per inch) of each image. Basically, when you take a digital image, you set the quality (or dpi) to high, so that when you print the images they look clear and crisp, not grainy. Well, an image on a computer screen doesn't need to be great quality to look fantastic, so, for an image you want to use on your site, drop the resolution down to 72dpi. The lower the resolution, the smaller the image size (in terms of bytes of information, not how big or small the picture is) and therefore it will load much quicker. If this paragraph means absolutely nothing to you, don't worry, use whatever image size you like, it will just take a bit longer for the page to display.

Be sure to remember to update the site after the wedding – there will be friends and family who were unable to make the day, so a selection of photos from your wedding would be very much appreciated. And *everyone* is going to want to see the all-important honeymoon photos, especially you posing on the beach drinking rum and coke whilst wearing your Speedos, you big, hairy monster.

Sorry, What Do You Want Me To Do About It?

Preparing for a wedding can become soul-destroying and all-consuming. Not so much for us blokes, but certainly for our soon-to-be wives. This will have an effect on you. Just as expectant and new parents obsess about their new arrival, often to an audience who are not at the same life-stage, the same can be true for the engaged couple. Your friends and work colleagues *are* excited for you both, but they've got their own stuff to deal with; they will come to the wedding and they will enjoy themselves – it's just that, well, they're not quite as intensely interested in the importance of gilt-edged invitations as you and your fiancée may be right now. Too much detail can be very boring to others. Worse, if the detail is also sandwiched between complaints about the hideous cost of the whole affair, you run the risk of making your potential guests feel awkward and guilty about coming – even though it was you who invited them in the first place. Do yourselves and your friends a huge favour and keep the moaning pretty much to the privacy of your own home – yes, it will drive the two of you to distraction, but your wedding will be all the better for it.

Those Hidden Extras

No matter how meticulous your budgeting, no matter if you end up using software products such as Microsoft Project, Excel and Sage Line 50 to plan your wedding down to the last penny, you simply won't account for everything. Sorry. I would like to say that the final bill should not come in as high as 20 per cent over, but it won't be far off. And that's the possible difference of a couple of hundred, if not a couple of thousand, pounds, all things considered. You *will* find a way to cover it, and if you've been that meticulous about the planning and the budget and it still comes out massively over, imagine your horror when you were faced with the final bill if you hadn't employed those techniques ... Be sensible.

Throughout your forthcoming preparations remember to compromise wherever you can.

Just Don't Ignore The Financial Controller

Cost-wise, weddings quickly get out of hand. We've already established that everyone will want to play a part – whether they're welcome or not. And for every person's involvement comes yet another cost that you hadn't even considered, never mind budgeted for. Budgets do go out of the window, but there should be a clear, public limit to your reserves if you are hoping to have a reasonably normal life after the big day. Don't just mindlessly accept everyone else's wishes and sign yourselves up to a debt-laden misery for the first five years of your married life. Be strong, be silent where necessary, and most of all enjoy the coming months ...

Ritual humiliation and
other rites of passage

The Stag

Best Man? He Was Until Now ...

You chose him because he's been there for you, through
thick and thin. He could be your brother, or your mate from
school, or simply the nearest bloke in the pub when you
decided to pop the question. The point is that you chose
this chap to represent you at your wedding. He's the man
that's going to make sure that everything goes to plan, on
the day. Not least making sure that the rings are there for
the two of you to exchange. He's the man who, should you
fail to show up, or die mysteriously on your wedding day,
will marry your bride-to-be, as tradition has it. He's the
man who is grateful for the honour, and won't let your
other mates forget it, ever, but deep down, he really just

thinks that this is a fantastic opportunity to arrange the most life-threatening, alcohol-assisted, ludicrously expensive, most embarrassing and dangerous stag do that has ever been staged in the history of groups of men with pockets full of cash and a passport.

Look at it from his perspective – what an opportunity. Only when the phrase 'stag do' is mentioned do many of us get the chance to spend a weekend away from our responsibilities, and only because it's a stag do can any of us possibly justify spending the best part of £500 on a trip to Amsterdam that is invariably going to lead to a headache for all, a night of tears for some, a sleepless night for two due to snoring, and an unwelcome STD for one …

Drink And Disasters

The rule that nothing that happens on your stag night is ever mentioned in polite society again should be something that is established from an early point. This isn't to protect the groom, who by and large will generally behave himself despite the circumstances, but should be put in place to protect the other attendees of the event. Take the example of the 'uncle of the bride', a man who's been happily married for twenty-plus years, getting rat-arsed in a seedy Amsterdam bar and deciding to join 'Sonia' on the pole-dancing stage wearing nothing more that his Union Jack underpants – it's deplorable and yet this sort of behaviour has become part and parcel of the quintessential stag night. If someone doesn't end up in the local nick, or end up with an STD a couple of days later, the whole night is regarded as an abject failure! From where has this rationale developed?

It is important to make the best man aware that

the stag night is supposed to be something that you would like to enjoy. Not everyone can afford a trip to Prague or paintballing near Manchester, so you should discuss with him the types of events you would like to happen and the cost factor. Most importantly, make it clear that you don't want anything dangerous or too embarrassing to happen. Stories of the unconscious naked bridegroom being stuck on the last train to Glasgow with a credit card taped to their head may be funny, but it's not something mates should do.

Get The Timing Right

In terms of timing, make sure it is not planned to happen too close to the wedding day, as too much expense and too many hangovers in the same month are not good. A meal, a few beers and a nightclub is actually fine, providing you have fun. If you think of the stag night as you would an event that you had to organize for work, then it may just give you the emotional distance to be able to decide how it should be planned. Fun is mainly what it is all about, but it also is an opportunity for blokes who will be together at the wedding to get to know each other. You may have your own set of old mates, but also want to bring along her male relatives, such as a brother or close male friends. But take account of personalities and make sure people don't feel left out.

Get The Preparation Right

A word of warning: stag nights can be disasters. One of my friends had a stag day and a mate, not his best man, hired a 'Gross-a-Gram'. A huge, middle-aged lady turned up and proceeded to remove her clothing, revealing her saggy topless form. This was the future bridegroom's idea of an absolute nightmare. He grabbed his wallet, shot off and apparently was nearly run over outside the pub. He wandered around in a mixture of shock and anger and contemplated dumping the stag party to watch a film about Algerian desert dwellers that was on in a cinema round the corner. He did come back later, but refuses to say if he would have run off if the stripper had been gorgeous. The best man can play jokes on you and show you up, but it must be thought through. Disasters happen when people start organizing extras off their own bat, to spice the day up.

When discussing your stag with the best man, do take some time to think about what might go wrong. You could get arrested first off. If you are drinking, and in a big group of blokes, you may draw a lot of attention to yourself, especially if you are in a loud and raucous group. Just because you have flown out to Barcelona doesn't mean the police won't lock you up it things get out of hand. Your planned evening can go wrong if some of the stag party gets lost or separated from the main bunch. This happened on one stag I went on, where outside a pub we split into two groups to go to a nightclub. It turned out that the bloke who was supposed to be leading us had no idea where he was going and led us on some wild goose chase halfway across north London.

Everyone must have a rough idea of the overall plan and what to do if they get left behind. Don't muck about between venues jumping in rivers, running in front of traffic, or climbing into a zoo. It's all bad and you may get refused entry when you get to the venue you are going to, or have an accident. Strip clubs and pole-dancing clubs may be fun – as may be casinos – but you can lose an awful lot of cash and they can also get quite boring.

The general rule is to have a simple plan. The more complicated you make it, the more can go wrong. It is also a good idea to do a general tour of your route a week or so before, or do some pretty good research if you are flying off somewhere. Some bars, clubs or restaurants don't allow stags. Others may only want your custom early on in the evening. If you are going on some kind of adventure day out make sure that you have the right transport and confirm the booking. Be sure that you know just how many people will turn up. Make sure you sit down and give your best man a list of who is invited along with all their contact details.

Don't Completely Overdo It
Without meaning to sound like your mum, beware of drinking too much or imbibing any other illegal substances someone may bring along. Being ill through drink is not fun at the best of times, and when it's your stag night you will get more free booze than you can handle, so you will have to pace yourself. If you do think of indulging in other activities, remember that you can get arrested or make yourself ill. If you are ill, then you may have to go home or even end up in hospital, so your best man should also be your protector – tell him you want to get home alive.

We have already talked about strippers and sex clubs. I know these are very popular, but they can also be a bit dangerous. For all the talk that you're sure it's all cool with your future bride, if she finds out that one of the party has had sex with a stripper on the floor of a Prague nightclub, then she will be seriously aggrieved, to put it lightly. By all means enjoy your night, but don't act the tit. A good night out can be a little bit naughty, but that doesn't mean it need be sordid. Remember the power of YouTube – being filmed on a mobile in an embarrassing situation is not cool, nor is it clever and within 24 hours it could be being streamed to millions of audience members around the world …

Last, but not least, if you are currently cohabiting with your bride-to-be (you sinner!), then ensure that you have made arrangements to spend whatever is left of the 'night' of your stag do somewhere else! Whether it is at a hotel or on a mate's floor, do not, under any circumstances, bring your drunken self and a whole heap of rowdy mates back to your gaff for a nightcap. Chances are you'll lose the woman you love and spend a week cleaning vomit from the bath, front and back gardens, and your cutlery drawer ... On top of that, the fantastic selection of Men at Work road signs, traffic cones and stolen women's knickers that made it back with you just won't fit in with the décor in the lounge.

So have fun on your stag, plan it properly and make sure everyone gets (to someone else's) home safe and sound!

Home Or Away?

Stag dos have become big business. Big international business – a load of not-so-drunken French, coffee-drinking their way through London's West End and a load of drunken Brits terrorising the population of Paris, spending euros like they are Monopoly money. On the flip side, it is still as popular as ever to take a trip to a seaside location and drink the night away in a large warehouse-like club, only to wake up on a floral-patterned sofa, with a knowing wink from the landlady of a rundown B&B. And then, of course, the latest wave of stag entertainment has to be the 'activity' weekend – tank driving, paintballing, go-karting, flying biplanes, a 'painting with watercolours' course; the choices are limitless.

No one destination or 'event' is guaranteed to be better than another, it all depends on whether the guests invited are up for the proceedings and happy to celebrate the imminent wedding of their mate – if you've got an *excited* and an *exciting* group of people, you are going to have a night to remember, even if you only end up going to your local pub. Whilst it will be the best man's responsibility to arrange your stag night, I have to reiterate that it is your responsibility to set the parameters – weekends abroad are excellent, but no matter how cheap the flights, add on the cost of the booze, hotels, transfers both in the UK and abroad, and all the meals that will be consumed, and a £20 return flight plus taxes to Barcelona can quickly turn into a £500 investment, per person! Be conscious and considerate of your friends' financial situations – very few mates will say 'no', whatever is arranged, but you don't want to leave them skint for the next six months, when all you are doing is essentially planning a booze-up.

The 'home' option is generally cheaper and easier for everyone involved and is especially welcome if your stag do is announced at quite short notice. Most mates will make the effort to be there and will make their own arrangements regarding somewhere to stay. The 'away' option is certainly perceived as more of an event, often with the 'celebrations' starting in the bar of the UK airport and not stopping until the return back to the very same rain-soaked airport 24 or 48 hours later. And finally there is the new fad of 'activity' stag dos. Don't be fooled into thinking this might be a less alcoholic option; far from it: you just might start a bit later in the afternoon – about 3pm rather than when the pubs open at 11am! I've personally enjoyed being on stag dos that fall into all three categories, but my favourite for all-round entertainment has to have been my brother's stag do, which involved an early-morning start at a paintball site followed by the bruised entourage visiting a comedy night at *Jongleurs* and then on to the pubs and clubs. As the mature, ageing bore that I am, I bailed out about 3am, while the rest of them carried on well into the next day. A great time was had by all and it won hands down over a night on *Las Ramblas* in Barcelona overlooked by *La Sagrada De La Familia* (there's a hefty service charge for that, don't you know!).

The Hen Night

You've seen them at it: a train of women all wandering from bar to bar following the leader with the learner plate round her neck; the obligatory wedding veil and the never-decreasing selection of alcopops in each hand. Total carnage. Although you may wish that your bride-to-be chooses not to attend a hen night, there's about as much chance of that as of you not going to your stag do ... so accept it. A bit of forward planning might be the order of the day – have the best man and the maid of honour communicate between themselves, ideally, so that you are celebrating at the same time in completely different cities (and maybe even countries). You can both get it out of your system, not have to face each other with horrific hangovers, and by Monday morning with at least a week before the wedding, it is done.

However you choose to do it, your stag do is sure to be enjoyable; just make sure you relax enough to treat it as a fun thing rather than an ordeal. And you know there will always be someone who makes an arse of themselves in a club, or gets totally wasted very early on and requires the constant guard of two members of the party, or who decides that this is in fact the most opportune time to express their undying love for you, throwing caution to the wind as they declare to the world that in fact they are gay and have held a flame aloft for you for the best part of five years ... the plonker!

From best men to
best venues

The Wedding

Phil: *I didn't know her family very well. I was also a bit overwhelmed by events.*

Simon: *It was really good fun. We made most of the wedding arrangements ourselves and my folks helped out.*

Neil: *We decided to hire a wedding planner, a project manager really, and they did the hard work and we made the decisions – easy!*

Andrew: *It was just a nightmare – everything went wrong and it cost a fortune.*

Everyone has a story about their wedding day: the car that

breaks down; the drunken relation making a tit of themselves on the dance floor and upsetting the bridesmaids. The accounts I got from my questionnaires were usually a mix of descriptions of how the day went, dressed up with a few amusing anecdotes. Ask a bloke privately for a bit of advice for the 'big day' and you will see him come over all vacant, then he'll give you some totally inarticulate description of how to hire a kilt or what not to say in front of the vicar. When it comes to wedding planning it is blokes who seem the least able to cope and who always have the most complaints.

Yes, we know marriage is a rite of passage, but many blokes, when they are talking to a mate out of earshot of the missus, will admit that it was a bit of an ordeal. Sure, a few may say it was easy and it was great and 'I was dead good, I was,' in just the same way blokes often talk about losing their virginity. After the event it's easy to say it was a great success, but if you'd interviewed them just before the wedding or halfway through the preparations, you'd have found they were worried about the venue, what to say in their speech, drinking too much beforehand, the event climaxing too early or not being able to perform later on that night – not to mention being more keen to find out what their mates really thought about it all afterwards.

What? Okay, let's get this straight. Men have invented magnificent machines and wondrous technology, cured diseases, commanded great armies, built fantastic buildings on every part of planet Earth. We have climbed the highest mountains and plumbed the deepest oceans, and even travelled to the moon. Yet when it comes down to the relatively simple business of organizing our own wedding, blokes can come a cropper. Oh yes, it's true. So let's look at why this is, and what might occur.

Your Wedding Arrangements – Made Simple?

What could be easier?

a: Book a state, public or religious building for a ceremony. Get a group of people (guests) to the venue at a set time to watch the ceremony involving you and your girlfriend. Turn up on time yourself and dress in smart clothes. Stand still during the ceremony – usually music/speech/ music/speech. Then, when prompted, give a set response you have practised beforehand. Kiss girl. Sign a form. Leave.

b: Get guests to the next venue where food and drinks will be available.

c: Arrange for set people (usually three blokes: you, your mate and her dad) to give speeches during the meal, which are basically formulaic in structure if not in content. Then arrange for music to be provided to enable the guests to dance, after first witnessing you dance with your new wife.

d: Get guests to go home or find somewhere to stay. Tidy up or pay someone else to tidy up.

e: Book a holiday (honeymoon) with your new wife.

That's it, boys. Not only is it not rocket science, if it was something you were asked to do for work, something without the wedding tag, it would be done in a flash without any gripes. So why the problems?

Who, Precisely, Is In Charge?
The question of who is in charge is at the heart of the issue. Weddings require a lot of compromise as you not

only have to agree with your girlfriend on any given thing, you will also have to get any decision passed through the control room of her family, not to mention the vicar/priest/registrar/ageing granny/best mate/hotel manager or caterer and your mum – it is this process that makes life difficult. It is difficult because you cannot simply *take charge*.

It is also difficult because you probably don't feel sufficiently knowledgeable about all the constituent parts that make up a wedding. Let's be honest, the reason you are reading this book is because you don't know what you are doing. Have you ever read one of those *Bride* or *Wedding* magazines? Didn't think so. Maybe you just had a quick scan through to see if this happened to be the month they were doing an illustrated feature on 'Sizzling wedding underwear that he'll thank you for, again and again and again'.

The best way to calm your fears is to have at least a rudimentary understanding of what is going on, so you can be more involved in the planning for it. And one way to do that is to get down to the newsagent's pronto and gen up on what's hot and what's not in the wedding world – at worst, you'll get some brownie points for taking such a pro-active step, which wouldn't be a bad thing. Then once you get more involved you have to bear in mind that dealing with wedding business is very different from dealing with work. Granted, you may have the attitude and confidence to ring up one of your suppliers at work and threaten to limit the blood supply to his genitalia if a delivery doesn't arrive the next day, but if you do that with one of your wedding suppliers, you're going to get in big, BIG trouble. Worse still, our loved ones often require us to place trust and responsibility in people we do not know, and sometimes do know, and whom we neither trust nor consider particularly responsible, i.e. our mates and her relatives.

She's Following Her Dream

First off, you can bet your bottom dollar that your future wife will have an almost perfectly formed idea of the type of wedding she wants. She may be flexible, but the point is she has doubtless planned and thought about it to the nth degree, then been to her mate's and her cousin's weddings and thought about it some more. How fixed or in-depth this may be is varied, but most blokes when asked what they want will answer something as detailed as 'in a registry office' and that is the true limit of their considerations on the matter, whereas their future spouse could have it planned down to the tartan-dressed pageboys and the reception in a specific hotel. These massive ceremonial, personal and social overtones are almost always focused through the glass of your missus's imagination. If you cannot come up with any alternative vision, then don't complain that you think that tartan pageboys idea is a bit rubbish; you'll just sound petty-minded and a complete spoilsport.

What is more, her parents are going to go all out to make sure she gets what she wants. Her dad may agree with you wholeheartedly that dressing up as a fairytale prince for your wedding will make you look ridiculous, but as far as he is concerned he had to go through it and so do you. She's his daughter and she will have her dream wedding (it's the final gift dad can give to his baby girl) and besides, can you imagine what grief his wife, your future mother-in-law, is going to give him and you if she doesn't get what she wants?

One respondent told a story about the planning for his wedding. He complained to a friend about his lack of input into his wedding plans. His friend gave him this advice:

'Look, it's a category 4 decision. Category 1, you get to do what you want. Category 2, you get to make major decisions, but you have to consult. Category 3, others have the final say but you are consulted. Category 4, you neither have a say nor are consulted.'

It sounds terrible. However, when pressed, he admitted to an element of exaggeration:

'I did feel that a great deal of what was decided was done seemingly over my head. But we did make the decision jointly about which guests were invited and we did choose the rings together and visited venues together. But I would have preferred something much smaller, and there was a lunchtime meal for guests who had not been invited to the registry office ceremony, which was not quite what I wanted.'

So perhaps the idea of us blokes being bullied into agreeing with all the bride's plans are a bit over the top. What is the case, as can be seen here, is that even blokes with their limited idea of what makes a good wedding often do feel strongly about what certain parts of the day should be like. These days, couples do decide most things together, and they should agree their wedding plans together, but often there is still the idea in a bloke's head that this is her wedding and that if it's her special day, perhaps he shouldn't kick up a rumpus. After all, it's a bit wet to get too upset; surely it's just about getting married and that's it?

Stand Your Ground
Actually, no, it isn't. If you do not stand up for what you want and feel that there has been a genuine compromise, then you are going to be upset about it for years to come. Yes, it is a very difficult and delicate situation, but you can

and must stand up for what you want. Her mum and dad may not like it, but you are not marrying them, and your girlfriend must compromise too. This is not about being an ungrateful arse and it really shouldn't become some power struggle where you are trying to show who wears the trousers, but if there is something you really feel strongly about, then explain why and be sure to offer an alternative solution.

This takes us back to the very beginning, doesn't it? When you first get engaged and start planning to get married, it's a good idea to think just a bit about what you would like to happen on your wedding day. DO SOME RESEARCH AND SOME PLANNING; IT'S WHAT YOU'RE GOOD AT! Then you can say, 'I would like to get married here.' 'I would like to wear this.' 'I would like the ceremony to be like this.' 'I want to invite this many people.' Don't wait till the plans are afoot and then get in a strop because you suddenly realize that you don't really want things done that way, after all.

Finding The Best Venue

So first things first. To host a wedding you have to find a place to have it in. Okay, you could just pop into a registry office, book a date, grab two witnesses off the street and you're done, but normally it will be a family event and that will require planning. What you decide to do, and what type of wedding you are planning, will of course be related to your personal wishes, beliefs and circumstances. But whatever you decide, you will have to book a slot at a church, registry office, hotel or dedicated site that hosts weddings; you can't just turn up. One of the biggest misconceptions people have is that you will be able simply to pick a date at your chosen venue, and then the planning will go from there. But if you are choosing a popular venue, even if you just want to get married in your local registry office, then you will have to book early. For any time between April and September for this year, and possibly for two years in advance, your chosen venue may already be heavily booked. Especially at weekends and, in particular, at bank holidays. So when choosing a date for your wedding, be sure you have the venue sorted first. BOOK EARLY!

Size Matters

Because a wedding doesn't just involve the place of marriage, but also a venue to eat, drink, dance and chat, not to mention hotels and B&Bs for people to stay, your job is to coordinate all this. You have to plan far enough in advance to make sure that your guests can actually come and, silly as it may sound, you must make sure that the venues you are choosing will support the number of guests you are intending to invite. A common mistake is to book a registry office or church that is too small to accommodate all the people you have asked. (If this does occur, get your mates (not hers) to sod off to the pub for an hour and bung them £100.) Luckily, many hotels and function venues are happy to support weddings and will have information packs and price lists and a nominated member of staff to liaise with you regarding your booking and plans. Obviously you are paying for all this 'special service' through the final bill.

Nevertheless, you should visit each venue and hotel. If you visit the registry office you will know what it looks like inside. Some registry offices look like a dilapidated Coventry curry house, while others look really lovely. Some churches are much smaller inside than they appear from the outside. Hotels can just be disgusting and really expensive. So do make sure you at least visit these places and, if the place you are thinking of booking is also going to supply the food, eat there too!

A Foreign Affair

Who said you had to get married in Britain or Ireland? More and more couples are choosing to take themselves (with or without an entourage) abroad. Combining the honeymoon with the wedding is pretty slick and although at first this might seem a bit callous, by flying abroad you are limiting the number of people who will be able to come out to the event – that's going to save you a fortune straight away.

A good friend of mine, Mark, took himself and his girlfriend off to Las Vegas without telling a soul (well, he told me because he needed to borrow some cash to pay for the flights). One week later, after they'd driven out into the desert in a stretch limo with their children and a pastor who was the spitting image of James Brown (I don't think they had paid for a themed wedding, he just happened to look like the soul singer), they returned to the UK as a married couple.

My brother chose to get married in Mauritius with only our parents as guests. Friends and family supported their decision and they still got presents – not bad going. The good news is that if you would like a foreign wedding, then there are numerous tour operators who will be willing to help you organize the event, and because of the specific paperwork and travel arrangements, the tour operator will essentially act as project managers/wedding planners on your behalf. Prices vary wildly for a foreign wedding experience and shopping around for different prices is highly recommended.

Bear in mind that because of laws in certain countries you may have to spend some time in the country before you are allowed to marry (usually four days to a week). Your travel agent will be able to fill you in on the specifics relating to your chosen destination. The wedding packages you can now organize sometimes include a bottle of bubbly, the all-important wedding certificate, a meal and a photographer, which means that the hardest part of organizing your wedding could be picking up the phone to give them your credit card number.

And Now For Something Completely Different

Most of us, of course, want to get married in Britain or Ireland. Over 60 per cent of marriages in the UK are now civil weddings rather than religious – weddings conducted at a registry office or at another venue that has been licensed for the solemnization of marriage. The number of approved licensed premises grows by the month and gives couples the option of getting married in places as varied as castles, grand country-house hotels and even football stadiums. This level of personalization and a wish to move away from the more traditional, formal church wedding and the less flexible registry office wedding have fuelled an ever-growing trend for genuinely unique wedding experiences.

Why the move away from the classic 'walking down the aisle'? Well, other than the chance to make your wedding unique to you, there is a definite move away from a church wedding just for the sake of it. We've become a nation of non-believers and the institution of marriage is seen more as a contract and promise between the two people it involves and less of a promise to a god. The choice of locations for a wedding can be an emotive one, and you and your partner may have very strong views on where that wedding should take place. There may be a lot of pressure from one or both sets of parents, if they have strong religious convictions, and managing expectations is going to be an ongoing concern for the two of you.

Registry Office

Function over form is very much the order of the day with registry offices. There are certainly a handful around the country which are pretty trendy, but the vast majority are extremely basic indeed. This is not to say that the actual ceremony conducted in the registry office will be any less solemn or important than a traditional church wedding; it just means you are removing any religious references. You will need to book well in advance, especially if you are hoping for a summer wedding on a Saturday afternoon. The beauty of a registry office wedding is the freedom you have regarding the actual service – okay, so you won't be able to do much about the drab waiting room-esque décor, but if you fancy a soundtrack featuring Orbital and Aretha Franklin (just like us) then you can have it. In fact, you can have anything you want, just as long as it has absolutely no religious connotations at all. (I'm still not sure how we got away with the seminal tune 'I Say A Little Prayer For You', but we did.)

One thing to note is that the experience does feel a little rushed – often there are weddings booked in forty-minute slots, so you really are in and out, then there's a quick photo in the 'garden' area and that's it, you're done. That said, we were a couple who had been living together for many years and who had a child together. The important part of the ceremony, for us, was the meal and the reception in the company of all those we care about and who care about us. Does a two-hour wedding service with all the pomp and circumstance make you any more or less married? No, is the simple answer.

If this is your chosen route, get in contact sooner rather than later and have some suitable dates in mind. Once you've booked a slot, you will be asked to come for an interview and you will need to bring proof of identity and passports, and answer some simple questions.

Whose House? God's House

This is the way it's been done for centuries and will, no doubt, continue to be done for centuries more, at least for a fair minority of the population. Church weddings are how many of us imagine we will eventually get married when we daydream as kids. Church weddings are how they're done in the movies and on the telly. In all the wedding magazines you won't see photo shoots of models in their white dresses posing outside the local registry office (next to the law courts and social services building). No, she will be posing outside a beautiful 17th century stone church. Churches are, generally, beautifully built and bring to the occasion a certain reverence and sense of tradition that definitely adds to the ambiance.

It is a dream of many brides-to-be to walk down the aisle and be wed in a church. If you are both regular churchgoers, then the likely venue will be your regular church, but you have to bear in mind its capacity. Friends of mine decided to tie the knot. He's Greek and she's Italian, they live in London, and each has enormous extended families, who all intended to be there for the day. The only venue that could possibly have coped with the staggering number of guests was St Paul's Cathedral! This is extreme, but the point remains: if you are booking a church for your wedding, be sure that all the guests will be able to fit.

On the flip side of this, some friends of mine weren't regular churchgoers but fell in love with a tiny chapel hidden in the Hertfordshire countryside. Quite simply, no other venue would do. So despite the capacity being less than 75, their entire wedding guest list was constructed around this immovable barrier. The basic rule is to find a church that is intimate, but not cramped. Don't forget that if you're considering decorating the church with flowers, then the bigger the venue, the bigger the expense. If you're going to want photographs (and let's face it, most of us do), then ensure that the church has at least a bit of greenery nearby so that your magical day isn't marred by photographs that make it look like you got married in war-torn Lebanon.

Be True To Yourself
As an aside, boys, you should bear in mind that whatever their religious outlook, a lot of girls want the walk up the church aisle in the big white dress. Now, if you have a real problem with this because of your religious views – perhaps you are a pagan and worship trees (seriously – it's a growing trend) – then you should bloody well tell your girlfriend beforehand. It is absolutely no good charging ahead with your own ideas for the wedding without taking into account the fact that your girlfriend is a (very) lapsed Catholic who nevertheless will want to get married in a Catholic church and who expects your children to be raised as Catholics. Of course, you've all discussed these matters at length already ... haven't you? Many blokes may be slightly religious, as in they'll say a quick prayer when being driven home on the back of their mate's Kawasaki 650 or when they are drunk and have done something particularly stupid. Many of you probably don't care either way. But this is serious stuff, with long-term consequences, and even if you are going to do the church thing just for the day or for her, don't get it into your head that you are just having a laugh.

More Tea, Vicar?
Chances are that neither of you willingly go to church, ever, not even at Christmas. Other than weddings, christenings and funerals, the only time you have set foot in a place of worship is when the excursion coach trip you booked on

your fortnight holiday to Seville decided to stop at a nondescript chapel in the mountains. The tour guide insisted that everyone on board got off the coach and had a chance to view some 14th-century mosaic tile work – thankfully followed by 17 bottles of vino tinto and half an octopus on toast at the local taverna.

But despite your absolute lack of religious belief, one of you has got it into their head (probably her) that a church wedding is the only way civilized humans can swear their allegiance to each other, and that means that the two of you are going to have to lie. Not just a little lie to your mate about how you can still manage it three times a night; or the little lie to your fiancée about only having four pints last night; or the lie to your boss about enjoying your job. Oh no. We're talking about cardinal sin here. You're going to lie to a priest. A man of the cloth who has dedicated his life to serving Christ, and you're going to tell this man (or woman) that you are a practising Christian; that you plan to attend church regularly; that you will instill the virtues of Jesus Christ into any children who will be the product of this holy alliance; that generally you both feel the need every now and again to shout 'Go, God' from the rooftops. Have you no shame?

The holy orders are onto you. You can't just phone up the priest or the vicar and tell him to get his glad rags on, you're ready to get married. Oh no, not any more. There are hoops to jump through, and jump through them you will if you want your fiancée to walk up that aisle. Your last contact with a vicar may have been at your primary school's harvest festival, or when your priest was called in as a character witness when you were up on a charge of disturbing the peace, but remember that this is his job. Actually, it's not his job; it's his *vocation*. Men and women of the cloth are under an obligation to consider your joint spiritual welfare and guidance. They are not some form of civil servant. They are going to perform a ceremony for you, but they are doing so as part of their work for the church, within their community, and they will have strong beliefs in the ceremony's religious, spiritual and familial importance for you. If you want to use the church as a venue, then you can expect the church to ask you to show some commitment and respect for it as an institution.

First off, you're probably going to have an interview at the vicarage – milky tea, custard creams and cucumber sandwiches (if you're lucky). You'll be asked about 'being new' to the area, even if you've lived in the same town for years (if you haven't been a regular member of the congregation, best to say you've just moved in!). You'll be asked to attend church at least six times before the wedding and if you're really unfortunate, like one of my interviewees, you may be pressurized into giving one of the readings at the Sunday service … Marriage, you are quickly learning, really is a big commitment.

Assuming all goes well with the interview and you manage to keep your Sunday appointments for the coming months, then you will be able to book a date for the wedding. It is a courtesy to invite the priest to the wedding lunch or at least to the reception as a sign of gratitude and it would be a wise move to leave a generous donation with the church to help with the-new-roof fund they always seem to be collecting for. Bear in mind that everything else is costing you money on your wedding day – the room hire, the food, the drink, so there's no reason to think that the church couldn't do with a few quid just because no one asks.

That's A Date, Then ...

The next big issue, and one which is inextricably linked to the venue you choose, is the date you decide on. If you haven't done so already, set the date as soon as you can. Even more important than that, tell everyone else what that date is and that you are expecting them to come! We're all busy people nowadays and, love you as much as I do, I've got two kids to think about, half-terms to handle, holidays to book, some work to do on the house AND only four weeks' holiday a year in which to do it. If you're expecting me to travel halfway across the country to see you tie the knot, I'll do it willingly, but play fair and give me as much notice as you possibly can.

The date you choose will have serious ramifications in terms of getting you what you want. There will be cost implications as well as the ability or otherwise of people to turn up. Choosing the summer bank holiday (the one at the end of August) is a good way to almost guarantee some lovely photo-opportunity weather, and that most people will be able to make it (assuming enough notice is given), and that the garden marquee will be a suitable venue. However, you will quickly find that a number of other couples have had exactly the same idea. They will have chosen the same venue, the same florist, the same photographer, the same church and the same bloody guests, at exactly the same bloody time.

Doing It A Bit Differently

There are huge discounts to be had if you break with convention and hold your wedding in the middle of the week, and there are huge savings to be made if you have your wedding in the middle of December rather than the middle of June. But this has to be a mutual decision, something that is acceptable to you *both* and, I suppose, your guests. We got married five days before Christmas, so the counter-argument could be that we were encroaching on an already expensive time of year for our guests. However, our counter-counter argument was that we and our guests would have spent money on meeting up at that time of year anyway, and the fact that we could combine 'a Christmas drink' with the rather exciting event of our marriage was essentially killing two birds with one stone. We saved a fortune on fees, everyone was in festive mood anyway, and most of our guests got out of their shocking office Christmas party with a legitimate excuse ...

If you're planning to be wed abroad, then bear in mind how wildly different the seasons might be at your chosen destination – yes, the web might show you temperatures in the balmy high twenties, even in October, but if you read between the lines you may also notice the 700 metres of rainfall per minute that comes hand-in-hand with that sun! There's a reason why flights to certain parts of the world are cheap during certain months of the year, and rain plays a major part in that financial algorithm.

Home or away, choose a time of year that suits your budget and suits your sensibilities – there's no point having a September wedding just to appease a few busy guests; this is your day and you should do damn well what you please. But if your budget is an issue, move the wedding a month or two forwards or backwards and see what effect that has on prices.

Sometimes You'll Need To Move The Wedding

A theme that appeared in a fair amount of the questionnaires was the very real need of either the bride, the groom, or both, to try and time the wedding so that it would be possible to include a certain friend or member of the family; either because a current illness would prevent them from attending in the immediate future, or, conversely, any long delay would result in them not being able to attend. In simple terms, there was a wish to either bring the wedding forward or to delay the wedding until a more suitable time appeared in the future.

This is an incredibly emotive situation and not one that this book or any other can answer definitively on your behalf. But just in case you need to address the situation and are not sure what route to take, I offer my thoughts.

A wedding is a time of celebration and the public declaration of your love – you will want your nearest and dearest to be there to celebrate with you. If that means you need to bring your wedding forward or delay it, so be it – the timing of your wedding isn't going to affect your love for your fiancée, but having everyone you care about to see you both get married is wonderful. If you've got to the stage of inviting people and then need to alter the dates, your guests will be very accommodating; likewise, if you are unable to set a date for the foreseeable future, that's fine too.

You Are Cordially Invited To...

So the venue has been chosen and the date is engraved in stone, now it's time to invite the guests. Traditionally, the parents of the bride send out the invitations, and that's fine if they're paying for it. But if not, you should send them yourself. It may seem a bit daft (because your fiancée has been talking to them both on the phone for at least an hour every day since you announced the wedding), but do send an invite to both sets of parents, even though it is taken as a given that they are both invited and coming. Parents like to keep this sort of thing as a memento and, given that they've agreed to fork out for the bar bill and the bridal suite on your wedding night, the least you could do is sprinkle some glitter into an envelope and go to the trouble of buying a stamp!

Be as formal or as informal as you like with your invitations – choose a format that sums you up as individuals and as a couple. We opted for the 'home-made on a computer' option. Given that guests were being invited to a registry office, followed by a curry house, followed by a house party, it seemed somewhat pretentious to go to the bother of naturally pulped paper pressed between the bottom-cheeks of Indian elephants steeped in freshly-squeezed lime juice and embossed in gold leaf – but I was tempted, I assure you. Obviously the formal, high-quality card invitations work a treat, as did a wedding invitation I received recently emblazoned with caricatures of my dear friends, Rob and Paula, drawn by a professional artist ... Each to their own. At the end of the day all that people really want to know is where, when and at what time. A text message or a cc email would do it, if you really wanted.

If you do decide to opt for a 'home-made' invitation, please understand that no matter how top-quality the bonded, pre-designed blank invitations may be, no matter how good the software and PC/Mac you are using, and no matter how good your computer design skills may be, 'home-made' will always look, well, home-made. We deliberately chose to challenge our guest's pre-conceptions of marriage and weddings with our arrangements (the registry office, the keg of beer in the bathroom, the curry, the no-presents rule, the marquee in December, the house party and, had I got my way, the karaoke challenge) and it was very important to us that the tone of the wedding was instilled right from the moment our guests received their invites – a kitsch look is what we wanted, and thanks to Microsoft Publisher, a kitsch look is exactly what we got. You set the tone for the whole wedding with your invitations and, therefore, you should regard the type of invitation you want to send with as much forethought as you will spend deciding upon your wedding outfit.

Be sure to include printouts of detailed maps showing the location of the wedding ceremony, the reception and where the hotels you have listed are in relation to the above. Most importantly, don't forget the RSVP stating a date when invites must be responded to. Keep the list of who is invited and tick off people who can and can't come, and also a reserve list of whom to invite late, if you fall short on numbers. Chase people up well in advance if you haven't heard from them, as the invite may have gone astray. (Or more likely they were too bloody lazy to respond.)

Spell It Out!

Whatever your eventual decision on invitations and how much you want to spend on them, the actual content needs to spell out the following, in no uncertain terms:

a: Who is invited? – Be clear (and correct)! It is of paramount importance that you check the actual spelling of everyone's name. Better to have an awkward phone conversation now than invite your mate's ex-girlfriend along.

b: What about kids? – Yes or no, make a decision and stick to it. If no, you need your head examined – not only will you be alienating some of your guests, you're missing out on the chance to see cute three-year-olds running around the place in pure excitement, not to mention the number of times they'll approach your wife at the reception and tell her she's a 'beautiful princess'.

If yes, do bear in mind that that also means very young

babies, who will cry. Kids under about eight have limited concentration spans. Yes, they will make noise in the church, yes, they will try to poke their fingers into the cake, yes, and they will refuse to eat the salmon starter you so graciously supplied ... They're kids, and you're not that long from being one yourself. Remember that kids get tired early on and only the older ones will be allowed to stay up beyond eight or nine at night. How you react to and interact with kids will also (unofficially, of course) be noticed by your bride – dance with a couple on your wedding night and you can expect an extra-special honeymoon, which could well leave you limping for months. Dad.

If you are going for the professionally printed option with your invitations, be sure to have the text proof-read before allowing the printer to commit to the print run – we all need editors, even authors (me more than most) – you simply can't edit your own work with 100 per cent accuracy. Have someone check for spelling, grammar and punctuation as well as checking the facts are, in fact, correct. This is not a sign of weakness or paranoia – it will be an expensive and embarrassing mistake indeed if you are inviting people to a wedding one week after it takes place!

If you're really on the ball, bearing in mind that invitations should be sent out at least 12 weeks before the wedding, then you might want to continue the same theme throughout all the printed materials you plan to use – have the same printer design your order of service, place names, menu cards and even the thank-you notes – printing at the same time will ensure a closer colour match and consistency of design. And that looks really, really slick.

Are You With The Bride Or Groom?

Choosing whom to invite to your wedding should be very straightforward. You have two families and two sets of friends. You have a fixed number of places available for people to attend. You decide on who is coming and you send them a letter asking them to come and they turn up. Oh, you wish!

The guest list is not just a list, it is a social anthropological demonstration of who's who in both families, and your seating plan is a physical representation of those various hierarchies, power relations and kinship groups in a geographical space – it's that serious. Get it wrong and there will be hell to pay. Once you start your list, you will learn things about her family and your own which will surprise you. Okay, you start with mums and dads, brothers and sisters, maybe aunts and uncles and cousins. But the further down the old relative list you go, the more complex it gets. Weddings have a dark underside; they bring together people who are related and who have known each other for years and therefore there are at least 40 years' worth of family feuds, problems, friendships and hatreds, all brought together in one place at one time. Add drink and nerves and, boy, do you get an unhealthy mixture.

When making your list you will have to decide on who will be coming to the ceremony and who will just come to the reception. There are obviously people who have to come to the wedding even if you don't want them to. For instance, deliberately not inviting your own brother, as you don't get on, is a truly terrible idea with long-term consequences. If you are not going to invite someone who may expect to be invited, you had better tread very carefully and let them know why you haven't in the most diplomatic terms. There may be people – friends of the family, ex-lovers or even ex-wives, whom you would like to invite but can't; invites can be tricky.

Are You In Or Are You Out?

In truth, deciding upon a guest list is not that easy at all. If it were solely your choice, you'd still be deliberating for months before finally settling on a list of nearly 700 people. Unfortunately, just to make the job even harder still, your fiancée is probably going to want to invite a few people herself (including her mother and 'annoying Sue from work with the stupid laugh'). And, just to keep you on your toes, as part of the unwritten contract you 'signed' when you accepted cash from your parents and in-laws to help with the cost of the wedding, they're going to want to invite a few of their mates too ... In the end, you'll be left with a long list that could easily fill the Royal Albert Hall and you will have to narrow it down, quite quickly, to the capacity of the venues you've chosen – say, 75 to 150 people. How is that possible without pissing a few people off? The answer is, it's not.

Now personally, if a mate said to me, 'I'm getting married, but I hope you understand, it's a small do and you're not invited.' I would be the first to say, 'No worries, I know what it's like, let's have a pint sometime to celebrate.' But experience shows that not everyone is as accommodating or understanding. It's *your* wedding, for goodness's sake. Not your mum's, not your in-laws', not your friends'. *Yours*. The two of you need to put your foot down, even if it means arguments and minor bloodshed. Every extra guest is going to add about £50 to the final bill – you're not made of cash and if you haven't seen such-and-such for two years since you left that company, it's probably best that you use an occasion other than your wedding as the catch-up opportunity.

It's difficult to fight back against the pressure from

parents and in-laws to include their golfing buddies and obscure second cousins whom you've never ever met. The capacity of the venue will always work in your favour, as long as it is quickly filled with your mates. Even so, you'll both still be asked to make room for Beryl, who babysat for you once in the mid-'70s, Gloria, who once did an Italian night-class with your mum in the early '80s, or Simon, who lent your dad a cordless screwdriver last week and has just heard about the wedding and is 'a right laugh', apparently.

What can you do? Well, you could just say no, not a chance, take your kind offer of money back; they're not coming. But that's pretty hard. Or you could say, fine, but at £50 a head those extra eight people mean we need another grand – take it or leave it. (Cruel, but under the circumstances, acceptable.) Or you could just add the names to the list, stick them all down at the 'stranger table' at the far end of the reception hall next to the gents, and readily accept that this is what happens at weddings. It's your choice ...

I Promise To...

There are statutory vows that you will have to say at your wedding for the marriage to be recognized legally – thankfully, if you're afraid you might forget them or fluff them, you are quite welcome to have the words written down on a card or to repeat the phrases after the registrar or the priest. Certainly, at least in registry office weddings, there is usually some scope to also incorporate any additional vows that are personal to you both. These can be specific promises to 'help with the housework' or 'always listen', or they can be more generic promises to 'support you in your endeavours' – it's entirely up to the two of you. Some couples like to incorporate a bit of fun into their vows, but these will have to be approved by the registrar. Be different and be daring if you like, but most of all be honest – you are promising to do these things, so they can't be flippant or throwaway lines, included just to raise a laugh from the guests.

Best Of The Best

And then there is the matter of choosing a best man – whilst avoiding alienating all your other friends ...

There comes a time in every man's life, once he asks his girlfriend to marry him, that he has to tell his mates. You'd think that this should be a painless, joyful experience. Lots of mutual backslapping, some kind words of encouragement, and a general overwhelming sense of appreciation and acceptance for your monumental life decision. How wrong you are ... The moment you let loose with this news, everyone is there gunning for the job. The role of best man is obviously up for offer and interviews are now taking place. This may not be how you see it, but that's what's going on.

Who Is The Best Man For The Job?

Choosing a best man is a really important decision. It is actually a very important obligation you are asking someone to undertake – you are choosing someone to perform a job, a complicated job. You may want your best, oldest mate to be your best man, but if he is a chronic alcoholic with Tourette's syndrome, he may be a bad choice.

Choose someone you are close to and someone you can trust to do the job. You will have to rely on them for support and for advice and they must be reliable. Don't be afraid to delegate; the popularity of having two best men is often down to a realization that two heads are better than one and that each may have something different to offer. Choose someone who is confident and nice and good at dealing with people. Someone preferably the bride likes or your family know. Don't choose someone who is going to humiliate you at the stag do or in their speech, or someone who will get totally drunk before the wedding, and especially don't choose someone who will make a right mess of the stag night plans.

There can be a lot of personal politics involved in choosing a best man. I was once surprised to be taken out for a beer by two mates, one of whom was getting married. After about ten minutes, the future bridegroom very earnestly told me that he had asked the other friend present to be best man. He was worried I would be upset. In fact it had never occurred to me that I would be his best man and it was nice that I was even in the frame. It was also nice that he was sensitive enough to visit just to let me know. Such choices can upset people and so be careful not to hurt feelings. In one extreme case I know about personally, a friend of a future bridegroom was so put out at not being asked to be best man, he proposed to his own girlfriend, arranged his wedding on the very same date as his now former friend's wedding day, invited pretty much the same set of friends to his wedding and even arranged his stag night to clash – weird.

You may feel obliged, for family or traditional reasons, to choose your older brother or another close relative. This can be a disaster. At a recent wedding I attended, the bridegroom's two brothers were involved – one as best man and one as a children's entertainer. The one who was performing the role of best man embarked on a 20-minute discussion of their shared early childhood with such dull reverence that people just gave up listening and started talking amongst themselves. Whereas the brother seeking to distract and entertain hordes of sugar-filled hyperactive children seemed like some slightly disturbing surreal drama inflicted upon the guests. The best man's speech is a time-honoured ritual, but it's also meant to be entertainment!

Overall, remember that being asked to be a best man is a bit of a double-edged sword. It is an honour, but it is a responsibility too. He is supposed to arrange the stag night and prepare the speech and will usually have duties either as an usher or a witness or as some kind of host at the reception. If you know that the guy you would like to be your best man is simply no good at organizing parties/events, then delegate it to someone else. And don't let the best man take on too much.

Filling His And Your Pockets
You really need to trust your best man, for several reasons. First, you're going to be handing him a wedge of cash that could easily end up behind the bar, resulting in a severe headache for you and for him. Second, he will be holding two expensive rings that could easily be pawned. And third, because he was on, and organized, the stag do – and he is about to make a speech about it!

The best man's role is really quite crucial to the success of your day. Come the morning of the wedding, you will want to distance yourself from all of the 'minor' incidents and requests that are going to occur over the following 24 hours. You have a very important role to concentrate on, and having random guests asking where the best place to park is should not be your concern. That's why you have a best man and a team of ushers. Your best man will need a roll of cash in his pocket to cover a number of expenses that are bound to arise on the day. If you're getting married at a church, then there will be costs associated with paying the priest. People will need taxis, and some suppliers will have required payment on delivery. Have the cash, or some pre-signed cheques already prepared, and give them to him in an envelope.

This is one of those small things that is worth preparing for in advance. On the day itself you do not want to be trying to get to the cash machine on the high street so that you can buy your mate a pint or two later on. You are going to get through a shed load of cash on the day and it wouldn't be outrageous to be carrying about 200 quid in anticipation of expensive rounds, packs of fags, and the irresponsible but inevitable sambuca challenge that is unofficially timetabled for about 11pm that night.

Ushers
There can only be one best man, but you'd still like your closest mates (and brothers) to be with you in the first row of the church and to be recognized as being more 'special' than the other guests. Ushers will be your eyes, ears and to a certain extent your mouth in the build-up to the wedding ceremony. Guests will want to know where they can park their car. They will ask if they are allowed to take photographs in the church. What's the best way to the reception? Who killed JFK?

Ushers need to greet guests as they arrive and direct them to the bride or groom's side of the church. They need to hand out the 'order of service' cards, tell people to turn off their mobiles, tell them to move their car so that the bride will be able to get to the church – they will be fire-fighting all the niggly little problems that crop up when 100-plus strangers arrive in one place together and don't want to appear impolite or pushy, so just generally mill around looking a bit lost and confused. The ushers are also useful at the reception to herd guests to the correct table, point out where the loos are and generally look quite dapper.

The Master Of Ceremonies (Toastmaster)

You can always hire one, but if you have a number of friends who are all gunning for jobs to do, rather than making everyone an usher, how about picking your mate with the big mouth as toastmaster so he can finally put it to good use! The MC's, or toastmaster's, role is really simple; it requires someone who verbally can get everyone's attention and who also has the physical presence of a bouncer. Guests will need directions to know what is expected of them and what is happening next – the MC will do just that. He will announce the arrival of the bride and groom, he will inform guests when dinner is served, when the bar is open, when the room needs to be prepared for the evening celebrations and, most importantly, announce the speeches and introduce the speakers.

Take Me To The Church, And Step On It!

Another thing to arrange is quite how you and your bride are going to make your big entrance. A popular option is to hire a vintage car, or some other form of elaborate transport, in which the bride will arrive at the church and the married couple will then use to get to the reception. Personally, we used taxis from the house to the registry office and back again, and then once everyone was assembled, walked from the marital house to the curry house for the wedding breakfast. To be honest, at 2pm on the last Saturday before Christmas, with all the guests dressed to the nines and carrying at least two bottles of champagne each, we probably drew more attention from passers by than a hired car with some bunting would have done even if it were stuck in traffic.

Certainly, the vintage car look works very well in

photographs where everyone is dressed very elaborately – there is something especially grand about the chaps in their morning suits posing next to a 1920s Bentley (be sure to ask for a black and white or sepia version of that shot). The biggest advantage with a vintage car (other than the fact that it makes you look quite dapper) is the space it affords the bride for her dress. And the fact that it allows for a far more graceful entry and exit than you would get from using the old Rover Princess that your dad insists on keeping. The cons, however, are that assuming all of your guests (and the groom) are on time for the wedding, then they're going to be sitting pretty in the pews as the bride arrives outside to an audience of two strangers – you know, the two older ladies who seem to be able to smell a wedding in the air and are happy to stand outside a church for an hour just to catch a glimpse of the bride, before nipping down the high street to St Mark's because there's another wedding on at three...

Granted, all of your guests will get to see the vintage car (or motorbike and sidecar, horse and carriage, helicopter, Roman litter, Challenger Main Battle Tank) when you both leave the church or registry office, but only for about two minutes before you take a left just after the phone box. The alternative? Thank your dad immensely for his kind offer of a lift in his Skoda, force him to have two pints for breakfast so that he can't drive, and ask your mate with a company Merc to do the honours instead.

The White Dress

Every woman wants to look her absolute best on her wedding day and the thought of weddings for many women manifests itself into one overriding obsession – the dress. If we, too, believe in this principle, then, by nature, the dress should be the single most important and costly item. For some of you there will be absolutely no compromise on the dress and she's getting what she wants, regardless of cost. That's great. What doesn't make sense to me is all of that expense to buy a dress that will only be used once and then stored in a box until maybe your own daughter decides to get married in some twenty-odd years. Even if you end up having five daughters together, and they all wear the dress, as a ratio of cost-per-wear that's still pretty expensive ...

It is of course possible to hire wedding dresses, which is far cheaper than buying, but it is by no means cheap. Or there's the Internet, and the option to buy dresses off eBay in particular. Hiring, or buying a used dress, is in no way a second-class option – I mean, who is going to know and who is going to care? If the bride looks stunning, which she will, what difference does it make? Other than the extra two grand you've got to spend on something else?

A good friend of mine got married in a dress bought off eBay (just one careful lady owner). Only minor alterations were needed to make it the perfect fit. Because she used the shop who were supplying the bridesmaid's dresses for the alterations, all the girls went to the shop for a fitting at the same time and it looked as if she was 'buying' her dress new. She wisely decided not to let anyone in on the secret of the true cost and origin of a made-to-measure designer dress. However, just because you are worried about escalating costs, and see this as one possible route to saving money, it does not necessarily mean that your soon-to-be wife will agree ... be aware that suggesting she goes the second-hand route is venturing into a VERY SENSITIVE SUBJECT, and make any possible hints with the delicacy of a foreign-affairs diplomat ... or better still, wait till she comes up with the suggestion herself.

Looking The Part – You, Not Her

And while we're on the subject of image, let's have a look at you. Sometimes it can feel like the groom is almost an unwelcome annoyance during the preparations for the wedding. All of the promotional materials you've (well, she's) been reading focus entirely on the bride. All the attention from friends and family has been about how well *she's* been coping. Everyone wants to know what *she'll* be wearing on the day, how *she's* preparing for the day – right down to a minute-by-minute schedule of what needs to happen on the morning of the wedding from six in the morning until she walks down the aisle.

In a funny way, you'll probably get caught up in all this focus on the bride too, to the point where you probably would have forgotten you were supposed to be going for a suit fitting on Tuesday, had an usher not phoned to ask for directions. It appears that your job in all this is to give the thumbs up on certain decisions and spend the rest of the time just smiling like a nodding dog.

Fight back – no, you're not going to suddenly declare that you'd prefer the bouquets to be dominated with yellow roses (bad move), because that would be terribly out of character and cause your fiancée to worry about your sexuality. But you could decide that you too would like to look your best on the wedding day, and you'll do that by putting in a little more effort than just a liberal helping of hair gel and a shave on the day. There's all this money being thrown around on hair, nails, lips and eyes, so why not get in on the act? All right, so you don't want shiny nails or rouge lips, nor would you let anyone near your eyelashes or brows with a sharp metal implement, but you could decide to do something about that blotchy, unloved skin. No amount of moisturizer on the morning of the wedding is going to fix the ravages of the last ten years, but a two-week course applied religiously leading up to the wedding could really make a difference – just think, those photos are going to haunt you for the rest of your lives, and right about now, with all the stresses (both emotional and financial) of the past few months, you're looking like death warmed up. Send your girlfriend to the shops to buy it if you're feeling a bit too manly to be seen in that particular section of Boots ... but do make an effort.

The same goes for your hair – for most of us it's a 'three all over' or a 'short back and sides', but whatever your preferred cut, you'll know that your hair always looks slightly better three or four days after the event, than on the actual day when the barber takes clippers to scalp. Bear this in mind and write 'haircut' into your diary in bold red letters. You don't know what shenanigans you'll be up to on the day before the wedding, so do yourself a favour and don't leave it until the last minute. And do not even contemplate going to a different hairdresser/barber for your 'wedding cut'. It's too much of a risk, you could end up looking like Gareth Keenan from *The Office* or worse, receive a skinhead so close to the bone you look eight years younger, two stone fatter, and have friends of the bride thinking you're on day release from HMP Parkhurst.

Captured On Camera

As you've both gone to so much effort to look dazzling for your big day, you are going to want that recorded for posterity. No married couples are really playing the game unless they make their house-guests, for at least six months after the wedding, sit down and look through 16 photo albums and watch three hours of wedding footage – that's probably why guests who are playing the game will always insist on you coming round to them for about a year after the wedding.

It goes without saying that your wife will look absolutely stunning on her wedding day; in fact, she looks stunning every day from the moment she gets up in the morning until she goes to bed. You, however, are a complete mess. You've forgotten how to use a comb, you only shower when you're told to and your idea of dressing up smartly is to tuck your t-shirt into your jeans and wash your hands.

Weddings do far more for grooms than they do for brides – because it is such a miraculous transformation. Blokes in morning suits look the business. Stand next to your best man and your ushers and you could be mistaken for a leading boy band. You'll want to capture this day because you'll never look as good again.

Finding a good still photographer and a camera operator can be tricky, unless your friends recommend someone. Everyone can use a camera, or a camcorder, but that doesn't automatically mean that the results will be any good. This is certainly one of the cases where you shouldn't pick a supplier purely based on price – pay more, a lot more, if you really like a photographer's portfolio of work. It will be these photos that will last a lot longer than your memory of the day; it will be these photos that everyone will want copies of, so get them right.

The most exciting and worthwhile photos tend not to be assorted guests posing in front of the church, or the staged shot of the cake being cut – although these photos are important. They will be the 'stolen' photo opportunities that really captured the mood. If possible, book your photographer for the whole day, from the bride and groom getting ready right through to the first dance (anything after that is going to have far too many drunk people flailing their arms in the air and looking a bit cross-eyed).

With a camera operator what you are looking for is the 'essence' of the day, with multi-angled shots of different parts of the day, edited together as a montage. There's nothing more boring (even for you and the bride) than watching the entire wedding ceremony captured from the back of the church with such poor audio quality that you can't even hear what's being said.

Don't forget, guests will be taking photos and .mpegs on their phones, which you can later incorporate into your wedding album. And you can always leave a disposable camera on each table for guests to use over the course of the reception.

How's The Bird Coping?

From the very moment that you proposed, she's most likely turned into a uni-focused, one-track-minded, obsessed, neurotic, shell of the woman you once knew. You still love her, and she loves you, but you can forget about a cheeky shag on a Saturday afternoon, because there's far more pressing issues to contend with. That's right, you need to choose which of the 247 fonts you would like to have embossed on your wedding invitations. And if you manage to sort that out before three o'clock, there's just enough time to pop into John Lewis to revise the wedding list. Weddings – a joyful time for all … Bollocks! Right about this time you're beginning to wonder whether just living together might have been the better option all round.

How Are You Coping?

Well, paradoxically, you are the epitome of calm. You're cool about the whole wedding preparation thing – there are weeks, if not months, to go, so what's the big deal? You've been asked to make a few phone calls, which you have done, and you received the information you required. Based on price, you've decided that photographer x is the right man for the job and you'd be happy to have the reception in a crack den, if that's what your fiancée wished. The only thing that is beginning to grate on you a bit is HOW MUCH FUSS EVERYONE ELSE IS MAKING. It's a wedding, for crying out loud, not Operation Overlord and the D-Day Landings. Get a bloody grip, will ya!

Unfortunately, it is this external pressure, with everyone else becoming stressed and irritable and demanding, that starts to rub off on you too. Eventually you yourself are becoming a bit flushed about the whole affair, not (I hasten to add) because you are worried about the proceedings but because everyone else is making such a big song and dance. The irony is, you get stressed about their stress and it just adds to the whole emotional cocktail.

So plans are boring, are they? Well, yes, but get them wrong and you risk spoiling the day of your wedding and embarrassing yourself and everyone at your wedding. Something we could all bear in mind during the stresses and strains of organizing a wedding is the following, courtesy of Stephen:

'Think about all the weddings you've ever been to and what you hated about them. Eliminate those elements from yours. Simplify, simplify – the best, most enjoyable weddings are just big parties. Don't make people stand around – you've invited them to be participants, not spectators.'

Emotions will become as stretched as finances over the coming months. A simple decision about choosing chicken or beef for the sit-down meal suddenly deteriorates into a stand-up row where you are accused of being a self-centred, revolting pig of a man who has absolutely no consideration whatsoever for your future wife's feelings.

You *knew* that her mother had a lucky escape from a band of marauding killer-chicks when she was visiting a farm in Norfolk and you are deliberately voting for the *chicken roulade* in a deliberate attempt to undermine her role as director of catering, and showing a complete contempt for her very generous gift of time and effort. Have you no shame, have you no heart? You're beginning to think that maybe this whole wedding idea is a complete waste of...

And it gets worse. Much worse. Just when you think that you are getting a bit of a hard time from the future in-laws, you decide to confide in your own parents, who then take the side of your enemy and join in the general chastisement of your slack attitudes with warnings that 'Weddings don't organize themselves'...

So, you are left with two options:

a: Take the decision that you are on the losing side and therefore join the 'winners' whole-heartedly and get totally wrapped up in the hysteria of the event, or

b: Come to the conclusion that as these minute details of the wedding are obviously of great importance to so many people, maybe it is you who are actually wrong to seem so blasé about it all, and as a result you *appear* to get so wrapped up in it all that you are welcomed back into the fold and normal service is finally resumed.

Either way, to ensure that there actually is a wedding, you are going to become more interested and knowledgeable about cut flowers and table decoration than you ever thought was humanly possible. You will spend evenings planning four different seating arrangements based on a: who knows each other already; b: a random boy–girl ensemble; c: who needs a bird/bloke; d: my mates versus her mates; and once that is decided you will spend countless hours sprinkling glitter and silver stars into wedding invitation envelopes so that you can secretly chuckle on your wedding day knowing that you personally forced every single person at your wedding (including yourselves) to roll out the vacuum cleaner the moment they knew the date of your wedding.

Of course, the truth of the matter is, you will remain pretty much stress-free, compared to your fiancée, for most of the wedding preparations. At the end of the day, picking one caterer over another, or one photographer over another, is a pretty simple process. For you the stress will mount when the deposit demands or, worse, the invoices, start rolling in. It is at this point that you turn into a dribbling wreck – a matter of weeks ago there were several thousand pounds resting in a dedicated savings account. Now you are into your overdraft and you've still got the majority of the bills to pay. Now you are worried. *Now* you wish you had taken your own sandwiches to work for six months. Now you yourself are beginning to twitch.

Those Pre-wedding Jitters

Those twitches will get bigger and bigger as the wedding draws near, and it is extremely common for blokes to go mentally AWOL. What do I mean? Well, somewhere in the back of the bloke's mind, as the date looms, are all the fears and insecurities about commitment and loyalty that you've been repressing for years and years – you know, along with the memory of the time you stumbled into a service station toilet as a child and were confronted with the largest, widest, longest and filthiest poo in the world – and when those repressed memories start reappearing you know you're in trouble...

You're engaged to be married to the girl of your

dreams, but you start thinking: 'Have I slept with enough women?' 'Should I have slept with Jane or Janet or both of them at the same time?' 'Have I drunk enough beer, or gone to all the football matches I want to see?' 'Should I have done the 18–30 holiday puke and bonk fest?' What is worse is that this occurs at the exactly the same time your relationship with the love of your life will become dominated by seemingly hundreds of dull plans and tedious choices, all focused upon The Wedding.

These dull activities include visits to possible hotels, registry offices, churches, restaurants and village halls. Endless shopping adventures, where, unlike the male preference to buy your stuff in ten minutes and get home in time for the match, you will have to discuss and negotiate the choice of cravat, and what colour buttons will go with what colour cufflinks. Oh, and let's not forget those evenings in, looking at the aforementioned wedding magazines and the evenings round at her parents' discussing finance, modes of transport, who will be and will not be invited (including the low-down on mad and bad relatives whom hitherto you had never heard of), as well as that laborious weekend away to her brother and sister-in-law's house in Nottingham ... Then, just when you think it's all tapering off, it kicks off again, and you find yourself having to decide on the style of wedding invites; the choice of flowers; the choice of which readings you both want; who will be giving the readings; times; dates and, heaven help you, the menus and seating plans.

It's All Scary Stuff, Mate!

This convergence of 'What have I missed out on?' and the 'I am going to make your weekend as boring as I can' wedding planning, is enough to make many men want to go completely wild. Blokes will start wanting to see their mates 'before we get married'; they will start actively trying to avoid their girlfriend. Football, cricket, rugby will appear as deeply important spiritual all-male activities. Then there's the drinking! Blokes often use the run-up to their marriage as an excuse to drink themselves stupid. No doubt this could be excused as de-stressing or self-medication, but it is both a symptom and cause of the FEAR of marriage. It is the slow, creeping fear that accompanies niggling problems, not dissimilar to the 'Is Pete going to find out I snogged his girlfriend?' fear, or the 'Did I pay that credit card bill?' type of fear.

Weddings, by their nature, entail being involved in a series of decisions and stages, which have consequences. As they are related to a timetable with a final completion date, this produces a growing anxiety in blokes, and as the day of the wedding draws close this anxiety can build to all-out panic. This anxiety is exacerbated by the fact that we may not be in control or may not feel in control of what is happening. This is when boozing can start to seem all-too-attractive: it seems to freeze time, numbs the old thinking process and, let's admit it, if your mates are all up for taking you out in a pre-marriage blitz, it will be good fun. But if you are going loopy from the moment that you get engaged, then that is going to be hard on your girlfriend and begin to make her wonder in a negative way about her life as your wife.

Don't Blow It Now

Let's look at it from her point of view. She has made the biggest decision of her life. She has chosen Mr Right and just when you should be sitting down and having fun planning the details of this wonderful occasion, Mr Right starts behaving like some 19-year-old lad who's on a rugby tour. Suddenly Mr Right is going to look like a bit of a dickhead. What's more, and what can end up as a total disaster, you might decide to go out on the town and start behaving like a single, free bloke; accidentally forgetting that you are neither and ending up on the pull.

In one horribly candid story I received, a future bridegroom who was out on the town bumped into one of his ex-girlfriends. She knew he was getting married and knew his future bride. One thing led to another and, lo and behold, what the Americans call a 'sex act' was duly performed behind the local church. Hungover and horrified by his actions, he escaped into town the next morning, only to bump into the ex with her current boyfriend, who compounded everyone's guilt by being congratulatory about the bloke's future wedding.

If you are tempted into the idea of shagging about before your wedding, this may simply be an indication of the fear of the wedding and responsibility that it will bring. It could also be an indication that you may be making a mistake and that you are not ready to marry. Either way, don't be an idiot.

Communicating and getting involved are key to solving anxieties. If you are worried about the wedding and becoming bored with some of the planning, then TALK TO HER, for heaven's sake. In the very near future, she is going to 'officially' be your life partner. You are planning to go through your life together, so speak to her and gain her support. If you are feeling claustrophobic and bored with all the wedding rigmarole, then plan some nights out and visit your friends, but stay in control. No bloke ever found the solution to his problems at the bottom of a pint glass or in a one-night stand.

An Ongoing Job

Okay, let's say you have now booked the church/registry office, the hotel and reception and hired a disco all for the *same day.* You have visited some places for guests to stay and made a list of room prices and contact numbers and websites. Let's say you have agreed upon menus and on table drinks, wines and soft drinks. You have contacted the car hire firm to get that horse and carriage to pick up the bride and the VW camper to take your mother-in-law to and from the church, to the reception and then home again. Don't think for one minute it will all go smoothly and you can forget about everything until the day. You must chase them up. You must check beforehand and stay in regular contact with the various venues and key personnel. Make sure that you don't irritate them by ringing up all the time, but keep your eye on the ball. There are lots of things that could go wrong. You are really going to have to be alert, right up to the big day itself.

And On The Seventh Day ... Your Pre-Wedding Countdown

As well as getting rid of your stag-night hangover, there's an awful lot to achieve this week to ensure that your wedding goes as smoothly as it should. As anal as it may sound, write a list, a very intricate list, of what needs to be done each day and by whom. Jobs for you, jobs for your fiancée, jobs for the mother-in-law and so on. This is your hit list. Mark each one off as it is completed and leave nothing to chance. There are still some suppliers who need paying, or they're not going to show up with your flowers, or your cake, or your mail-order Russian bride. Sort it out!

Your Hit List

Monday If you are planning to go on your honeymoon within 48 hours of your wedding, you really need to pack now – you won't be thinking straight after the wedding and you really don't want to turn up at the airport laden with sharp implements in your hand luggage, strange liquids in bottles that you're not prepared to taste in front of a Customs officer, and no passport. To be honest, blokes find packing really easy; some undies, some socks, some shorts and a few t-shirts and shirts. Throw in a pair of trainers and a pair of flip-flops, a fleece for when you get home, a toothbrush and the latest Dan Brown novel, and you're sorted. Your fiancée, however, will need to really think about what's coming and what's not. This all takes time. (Weeks!) If you're getting married on Saturday and going abroad on Sunday, then you're already leaving it a bit tight thinking about packing on the Monday before!

Tuesday Make sure you've organized the upfront payments due for all of the services you require, or they're not going to arrive! By this stage there should only be the venue bar bill to cover and possibly the photographer's, who will want the rest of the payment on delivery of the prints and negatives. Ideally, you will want to settle your hotel bill (for rooms) before the event, because there seems to be a rather worrying trend for hotels to charge the bride and groom in advance for a particular room you've agreed to pay for, and then try to charge the occupants as well! Get everything in writing and bring your folder of receipts with you on the day.

Wednesday If you've opted for a church wedding, then you'll no doubt have to have a rehearsal at the church. This can take all evening. If not, then you've still got to sort out the seating plan (again), work out why your hire suit doesn't fit (you haven't been a 32-inch waist for years, you fool) and confirm to the caterer just how many meals are required and how many of them are vegetarians (it will cost you, but always budget for at least two extra veggie meals, as there are some guests who will expect you *just to know*, even though they're friends of your fiancée and you've never met them before).

Thursday This is your last night together as an unmarried couple and, just as it with exams, what you don't know now, you'll never know. You could decide to wear an all-in-one rubber suit with matching gimp mask and declare to your beloved that this is how sex is going to be from now on – just to get a reaction ... and after you've been kicked in the goolies you can admit it was all just an ill-prepared joke, sorry. Talk to the best man to check he's written his speech, as well as to confirm that he is coming out for a pint tomorrow night.

Friday... The daytime, which you've sensibly booked as holiday from work, will be spent driving round like an eejit picking up cakes, flowers, clothing and the cufflinks and new belt that you're going to need for the big day, as well as purchasing the various gifts for grannies and bridesmaids that you forgot to buy in advance. If you failed to book a haircut in advance, you'll rush to an untried barber and you'll now be at home looking in the mirror wondering whether you'd be better shaving off what's left with a Ladyshave...

... D-Day Day becomes dusk and it's over. You're now forbidden from being in the same vicinity as your bride-to-be; her friends arrive and you make a genteel exit. (There's now so much oestrogen in your house, you're positively running out of there.) Meet up with your best man, friends, family and mates and have a lovely evening ...

The Night Before...

All the guidebooks, your mum, even common sense, will tell you it's best to have a big meal, a nice bath and an early night before the big day. If you're playing by the rules, though, the chances are you'll be staying somewhere other than your own house tonight, as you currently already live with your fiancée and you're not supposed to see her until she walks down the aisle. So in all likelihood you'll be in a hotel somewhere accompanied by your best man, if not your entire family and some mates – and they're all going to want to get horrifically drunk, with you.

My night before was also my birthday (a shrewd move so that I would never forget my wedding anniversary), and after a day spent erecting a Glastonbury-esque aluminium stage-frame marquee over the decking/garden, I was up for a pint or two. We did have a few bevvies and we did stay up into the early hours catching up and talking crap, but come the next morning I felt on top of the world – bright-eyed, bushy-tailed and so full of adrenalin that it bitch-slapped any residual alcohol in my system so far away that I couldn't remember the taste of beer. And I suspect the same will be true for you too, as long as you don't deliberately try to drink more than you have ever consumed in your life before.

The important thing to remember is to do what you would normally do to relax. For example, I never take baths (not because I'm an unclean freak, I just prefer showers), so the act of bathing for me would be completely alien and wouldn't have the desired effect. I also feel relaxed around friends and family. And so an evening of catch up and rhetoric was a fantastic alternative to a lone early night in a soul-less hotel room.

The great thing about the 'night before' is that you will probably feel totally at ease with the prospect of marriage – nay, looking forward to it – as the nerves have yet to kick in. With Buddhist-like calm you will wow onlookers with your wit, anecdotes and general wellbeing, despite the apparent stresses you should be under. Enjoy it, bask in it and know that you're completely safe until about two hours before the guests start arriving at the church or registry office ... Nerves are nervous to put in an appearance too early, in case you beat them off before the actual event. Then they build and build until they reach an absolute peak when you are at the venue, waiting for your bride to appear...

Every Groom's An Island

There's standing at the front of class feeling like an idiot because you got the question wrong, and there's standing at the front of a church waiting for your bride to arrive. Both are terrifying and both will give you shudders every now and again for many years to come, and no one else can really understand the torment. Not your best man, not your dad, not even if they've both been through the experience themselves – this is one man's personal pain being played out in front of everyone you know and care about. How scary is that? No, you won't faint, no, you won't have to rush off to the loo to poo or be sick; no, your flies are fine, as is the cravat you keep fiddling with... Yes, she is coming, yes, she will look wonderful, yes, you are doing the right thing, and yes, she will marry you ... It's just, as you stand in the pew nervously checking the back doors of the church and your watch (whilst nodding and smiling at guests as they arrive and take their seats with such carefree abandon), your mind and nerves are working overtime to try and convince you to run out of the side door and take up orang-utan conservation in Borneo, never to be seen again.

You're cacking yourself about everything. You're nervous about sealing the relationship with the woman who means more to you than anyone else in the world. You're nervous because you are worried *she's* made a mistake, that you're both delusional and got a bit carried away in the moment of it all; you suddenly feel you're not old enough, wise enough, mature enough, stable enough to become a husband to this woman, and she is as mad as you are to even contemplate the idea ... and then the doors open and the organist kicks in with that goose-pimple-raising chord that can only mean one thing ... she's here!

I think that most of the stories of grooms being left at the altar are just that. Stories; fictional fantasies – mainly because no one who has spent so many hours preparing for a wedding is going to want to bail out at this stage. The main reasons for brides being late are the usual make-up/hair/nails crises, or punctures and engine failure, or last-minute tears (of joy). And, as you well know from your commute to work every day, that particular A-road is a complete nightmare. You haven't been abandoned and you won't now have to choose between the frumpy bridesmaid and the goofy one – it's just that the bridal car happens to be stuck in traffic.

And then suddenly she's there, the ceremony is starting, you're on the verge of getting hitched. All those months and months of planning culminate in a service that seems to pass in the blink of an eyelid ... and then it's straight on to the reception...

The Reception

Champagne, sugary
cake and speeches

So, the official bit is over and you're now a married couple. Incredibly, very soon you'll be halfway through the day that has consumed you for the last six months. Someone slow everything down!

That post-service glow is pretty hard to beat. Your cheeks are hurting from the grin that's plastered across your face and your wife is looking absolutely beautiful. (You won't be the first brand-new husband thinking that it would be great to sneak off to the room with your wife for 20 minutes, but that isn't going to happen. Sorry. Good idea, though.) You're feeling on top of the world ... There's only the small matter of feeding 100 people and then, of course, your speech. But hey, that will be over as quick as the wedding service and before you know it, you'll be showing your guests your *MC Hammer* moves on the dance floor. So take a seat, have a glass of wine and let the party begin....

The Venue

Where you choose to have your reception, and in particular the capacity of the venue, is something you need to decide early on, because that is going to determine how many people you can invite. Hotels remain the most popular choices. They are expensive but they're geared up for it, with some being licensed for weddings too, so it can become a one-stop shop for you and your guests, especially if everyone books rooms at the same place. Don't forget to consider country houses, sports clubs, funky restaurants or even bars and clubs. Choose a venue not just on capacity, but on how it works for you as a couple.

Some good friends of mine, Fil and George, wanted a reception to remember. Bearing in mind that half of Sicily and Cyprus were flying in for the occasion, they went for somewhere central, large and very special. So, for their reception they decided to book a rather trendy venue in London. Then, a matter of weeks before the event, this venue informed then that they were double-booked and couldn't do their wedding after all. (It transpired the extra booking came from friends of the Beckhams – it's not what you know, it's whom you know...) So said venue (after much complaining from Fil and George for ruining their plans) offered to pay for their reception – well, the only place available on the day was the Savoy! Understandably, the guest list went up to 250 people. Everyone arrived at the new venue and a glorious day was had by all, not least because they enjoyed a five-course meal, free drinks all night for everyone and the bill (paid by the original venue) came to about £60,000! What a result.

Let Sleeping Guests Lie ...
Ensure that the more volatile members of the wedding guest party have booked into the nearest hotel to the

venue. Hopefully, their room will be directly above the venue you've chosen for the reception party and therefore they can stagger up to bed with a stolen gin and tonic in hand and sleep it all off … while you will be booked in to the bridal suite on the other side of the hotel, well out of earshot and influence of their nefarious nocturnal antics.

Down At The Social?
Maybe it has a certain ironic, naff appeal, but really, this should be a last resort; trestle tables used for the buffet, guests sitting on mismatched plastic garden furniture, the makeshift bar stocked with rusty cans of lager and bad wine and a children's entertainer-cum-DJ to get the party started. Honestly. You'd be better off halving the guest list and putting on an intimate house party instead.

Garden Party!
Hopefully the weather will be good, and even if it's not, a marquee in the garden is a fantastic venue for a wedding reception. Bright, airy, the smell of a freshly mown lawn, it really is the quintessential English way of doing things.

If you're in the generous position of being able to supply all the booze, then you will be much more in control of the cost, of both your own and your guests' expenses, because you will know that the guests aren't being fleeced for over £3 a pint at the bar. You are making sure they're fed and watered and won't have to put their hands in their pocket all day – and they will love you for it – and they will probably show their own generosity in terms of your wedding present if this fact is made subtly clear to them in the invitation.

Or, All Back To Yours ...

And then there's the humble house party. Our chosen venue for our wedding reception; 75 people in a four-bed semi all having a fantastic time and proving to be the best night of my entire life. You and most of your friends and family will feel incredibly 'at home' in your house. There isn't the awkwardness of a hotel room that's 'been done-up' for the day. You'll have all your favourite tunes close to hand, your favourite glass to drink out of, and it's not going to cost you anything to hire it!

Despite fearing the worst, the only damage done was the best man stumbling, nay, collapsing spectacularly onto a box of glasses, thereby causing a few breakages. I've broken just as many on an evening whilst trying to do the washing-up after a few beers!

For the music we hired a DJ who was a friend of one of the guests; this way we had a recommendation that he was good and it meant that none of the guests was stuck with a 'job' to do all evening.

Feeding The Five Thousand

People like to eat, and that's a real shame because if they didn't you'd be able to shave a fortune off your wedding bill. Sadly, that's how it works. It is something socially ingrained in all of us to want to share a meal with those we love and care for; we go out for romantic meals as couples; we share large meals with our family during various festive seasons and it feels like a very alien experience indeed to eat by yourself ... so a 'wedding breakfast' is in a way the most important part of your wedding. It's where you can share a meal with everyone you hold dear, to celebrate your wedding in the best possible company, even if you all happen to be scattered around 20 tables. To feed someone is to keep them alive and there is no greater gift than that. However, as benevolent as you might want to be with your life-saving generosity, catering for a large group of people can be very, very costly.

Seasonality should play a major part in what you plan to serve your guests – the last thing anyone wants on a hot summer's day, whilst wearing a suit or a posh frock, is to be faced with a full roast dinner, boiling-hot gravy and a heavy dessert. A barbeque and a selection of salads, however, could be just the ticket ...

A sit-down meal is by far the most popular way to celebrate a wedding. Obviously there's a high cost, but you're paying for the kitchen staff and waiting staff to look after everything. With most meals of this ilk, there will be a set menu of a starter, main course, desert and coffee. You will have to advise the venue of how many vegetarians, demi-veggies, no-red-meat eaters, vegans, lactose-intolerant, nut-allergy sufferers and general fussy buggers are coming, and cater accordingly – or you could just ask those guests to bring a packed lunch! Usually, when choosing the menu the advice is to steer clear of anything too rich, too creamy or too spicy so that the meal has maximum appeal to as many guests as possible, which doesn't actually leave you with many options – I personally feel that this is pandering to the minority because all of our friends pretty much eat the same as we do. So, you could just choose your ideal dish and offer a bland alternative for the minority. One thing to remember, no matter which venue you have chosen, is how difficult it is to plate and serve over 100 meals so that they all arrive at the table piping hot and at the same time. There's no real way of improving the technique, so if your meal arrives lukewarm, then rest assured it is cooked through ... or is it?

As ones who occasionally practise what they preach, my wife and I chose to have our wedding meal at a local trendy curry house. It was absolutely fantastic – the red-blooded meat eaters got what they wanted, the white-meat aficionados got what they wanted, the veggies were in seventh heaven and my dear old nan got scampi and chips. Everyone was happy, it was the nicest curry I've had outside Nepal and we were allowed to pay a one-off fee of 50 quid corkage to bring all of our own wine and bubbly, which saved us a fortune. Plus, as we'd eaten there before, we knew exactly what we could expect, which was a huge worry off our minds.

The cheaper alternative to a sit-down meal is to have a sit-down buffet. The food can be served hot, cold or a mixture of both, and you will only need a fraction of the staff. The beauty of a buffet is that everyone gets as much as they want of everything they want. If they're planning a bit of a session they can get second helpings and the whole affair feels a little less formal and cramped compared to many sit-down meals. Guests have the chance to go up for food as they wish and any kids invited will eat far more 'finger food' than they would had a three-course meal been served. Buffets are losing their stigma of being cheap (because they're not!) and cheerless – obviously you'll get no marks for mistaking this for a child's sixth birthday party and supplying only egg-mayonnaise butties, sausage rolls and crisps; but a well-balanced selection of foods including meats, salads, rice and couscous, pasta dishes and hot or cold vegetables (and sausages-on-a-stick because everyone likes them!) will go down a treat, especially when combined with a staffed barbeque.

We Want The Finest Wines Available To Humanity

Think wedding – think booze. Whether you are a big drinker or not, weddings tend to be very drunken affairs for all concerned. You won't be able to control how much people drink on the day, but you can control how much it will cost you.

Most couples (or your or her parents) will want to contribute something towards the alcohol requirement for the day and the easiest way around this is to come up with a figure and see what that covers. If you're planning a 'wedding breakfast', which is actually the big meal at the start of the reception and is more of a wedding lunch, then you'll be looking to provide both red and white wine on each table (about half a bottle per person, or, if your friends are anything like mine, at least a bottle each). You should also provide at least one glass of something that fizzes for the toasts, and some bottles of water (still/sparkling) for each table. Some soft drinks for the kids and the losers of the 'I think you'll find that it's your turn to drive, darling!' tussle wouldn't be a bad idea too. That's the basics taken care of, but most guests will be drinking a little bit more than that, and here is where the costs start to escalate.

Bring Out The Bubbly

It is also nice to provide a welcome drink as guests arrive at the reception venue. It might be a while before the formal sit-down meal commences and so a glass of bubbly/Buck's Fizz (or Pimms works pretty well too) would be a welcome treat as everyone mingles.

Make a provision for a few extra bottles of wine to be served during the meal and the more sparkly that's on offer, the better. For a nice touch, you could also provide a bottle of port and/or brandy to accompany the coffees, as people settle themselves down ready for your wonderful speech.

Then there's the question of the bar, both before and after the meal. Very few couples, or even parents, will agree to picking up the entire bar bill (it is more manageable if you are planning a marquee wedding because you can buy all of the booze wholesale and bring back whatever isn't used). If you are using a venue bar, then by all means leave some money behind the bar, but remember that if everyone has two drinks – say eighty guests at £3.50 per drink – that still adds up to £560. I also suspect that through incompetence or even dishonesty, the bar tab is not treated by staff as 'proper money' and there's no real way for anyone to prove that the full tab has been spent before the free bar becomes a cash bar ... Sadly, certain guests will take the piss (usually the blokes, I'm sorry to say) if they get wind that there's a free bar (or money behind the bar). It's absolutely disgraceful, but I've witnessed it a few times myself and interviewees complained about it in their responses.

In one case, Rob, a good friend of mine from university, generously put hundreds of pounds behind the bar, thinking that everyone would get a couple of pints each at least. What actually happened (unbeknownst to him at the time) was that a cousin took the opportunity to order three bottles of expensive champagne for his table – at £90 a bottle – and with a couple of other 'guests' ordered triple vodkas and Aftershocks (before the meal!). There was very little left in the pot for the other 99.9 per cent of guests. Stern words were spoken after the event, but Rob felt he'd let his friends down because they had to put their hands in their pockets before the speeches had even been made. We didn't mind too much, especially on learning that someone had taken a wee in the cousin's pint and someone else had tapped off with his bird in the car park! That's karma for you.

The thing to remember about alcohol and weddings is that people will always have a good time and they will always drink too much – regardless of whether you pay for it all or not. In our case, for our reception that we held at our house, we asked our guests not to buy us a present, but instead to bring a bottle or two. We bought a £200 stockpile of lager, wine, mixers, fruit juices, fruit slices and ice. I also managed to hire a keg of real ale from my local pub and by the time the last guests left (four of whom had spent the entire day and night drinking only champagne), we still had enough booze left over to mount another major party later in the year.

Time For A Booze Cruise

Another great idea if you're planning a reception at home, or in a marquee, is to take a booze cruise to France to stock up on your wines, beers, spirits and champagne – get the best man involved, hire a van if need be, and be sure to book a night in France so that you can actually 'sample' a few of the very many choices available. It's a great excuse for a 'free' holiday and in between deciding which 70 litres of Burgundy to buy, you can finalize the finer points about the wedding!

The Seating Plan

Whatever type of wedding breakfast and reception you plan, chances are you will have to arrange a seating plan. This can cause far more heartache than is really necessary. There are hard and fast rules about the 'top table' which basically mean that you and your wife will be flanked by your respective parents, grandparents, siblings, your children, if any, the best man and the maid of honour. If your or her parents have since re-married, then you'll have to make decisions about who sits next to whom and keep an eye out for any sharp implements.

Fancy A Mingle?

Regarding the rest of the guest list, you need to make the decision of whether you want to acknowledge cliques or whether you want everyone to mingle. The clique option is to simply realize that you both know everyone in the room, but all of your guests only know those from one particular part of your life – family, school, university, work, neighbours. So, if you stick all the people you shared a house with as a student on one table and all of your uncles and aunties on another, you know that your guests will be grateful for a chance to catch up and chat among themselves – the only group that this might not count for is work colleagues who are probably sick of the sight of each other and would rather take their chances sitting next to your relations than continue 'water-cooler chats' about the redundancies planned for later in the year. Once everyone's loosened up a bit thanks to the wine and food you so generously supplied, you hope people will mingle when the tables are cleared and the music/entertainment begins.

The alternative, and the one that takes the time to plan, is the mingle option. As you both know everyone in the room so well, you may have subconsciously thought that Amanda from work would really get on well with James from university, they're both single, and ... yes, you're matchmaking your mates and will try your best to place potential couples together, as well as trying to encourage cross-pollenization of conversation by introducing people to each other who would not normally meet in the outside world.

There are many ways to organize this, and none of

them are quick, but the most effective is to clear a space on your kitchen table, use A4 sheets of paper to represent each of the tables planned for the wedding breakfast, and use Post-it notes with each guest's name on one. Assuming you have 8o guests sitting round ten tables, start by placing an 'alpha guest' at each of the tables; this will be a person who is a confident conversationalist, a joker or a relation. On the same table, but not necessarily beside the alpha person, place their partner. If the alpha person on table four is one of your work colleagues, then place another work colleague opposite them on the same table (and their partner) – this way, if mingling just really isn't happening, then the two colleagues can converse across the table. Introduce their partners, and you've got four out of eight people talking, which will encourage the others to join in. Follow this pattern around the room so that, to the best of your ability, it is contrived that everyone knows (or knows about) one other person at their table. If the plan works, then each table should become a buzz of conversation, followed by the swapping of mobile numbers, followed hopefully by some heavy swapping of saliva a bit later on the dance floor.

There will always be one guest who, for whatever reason, is coming alone and knows only the bride and groom (person Y). If you are aware of this, take the time out about ten days before your wedding to invite this person along to your house along with someone else who will know lots of people at your wedding (probably same sex so that there isn't any awkward 'This is a set-up' feeling – unless, of course they're both gay, in which case it could seem like a set-up ... or, of course, unless you do want to set two people up...) Anyway, if you're clever with your seating, these two new acquaintances will 'meet' again at the wedding and person Y is no longer a gooseberry.

Clique Clique

The mingle plan is admirable but from my experience of attending weddings employing both tactics, I think the clique method works the best, mainly because as we get older it becomes increasingly difficult to meet up with friends from our past regularly, and that old adage about only meeting up at births, weddings and funerals starts to look all too true. Well, this is one of those occasions, and as a guest who went to university with you, I am looking forward to congratulating you on your wedding day and then catching up with our mutual friends. And if I am keen to mingle, I will. You don't need to sit me next to your fiancée's mate with the big bazookas for me to notice her. If I'm keen, I'll make my move on the dance floor ...

The other thing to consider is if you have invited guests with small children. Then it's usual to place them near the back and near the exit/toilet – parents will both understand and thank you for your foresight. Overall, you should try to construct table plans in a balanced way. Plan as best you can to put people together who will be comfortable with each other, so that you create a friendly environment (and keep people apart who don't like each other!). Don't stick some old granny on a table primarily full of young lads, for example; they'll try to be cordial at first, but as the wine flows the language will become more and more flamboyant – not what she needs to hear at 92 years of age. Remember where there will be access to loos, particularly for the young and old, and where waiters and waitresses will be walking about with trays of hot food.

Food That Entertains

There is a concern among brides and grooms that their guests will become bored during parts of the day's events.

Not at all. Yes, certainly some entertainment is expected at the evening reception – be it a DJ, a karaoke event (I *so* wanted that, but was vetoed...) or a live band – but don't feel that the whole day needs to be micro-managed. If people are eating, then that's what they will be concentrating on; in the minutes between courses they are quite capable of small talk, if not of deep, in-depth political, religious and general 'putting-the-world-to-rights' rants, all dependant on how free-flowing the booze has been thus far. To go to the trouble of a string quartet while people eat is probably overkill. Granny will like it, but most people won't notice.

However, a friend of mine still felt the need to provide entertainment towards the coffee-serving stage of proceedings that would also double up as a 'speech warm-up act'. He chose a live entertainer who walked amongst the tables singing the classics and interacting with various guests – the wine flowed, Aunty Mable found her true baritone voice, and by the time the top table began clinking glasses for everyone's attention, everyone was so hyped up, they were actually preceding the speeches with applause and cheering ...

Lend Me Your Ears ...

Which brings us to the speeches. No matter how many books you buy, no matter how used to public speaking or presentations you are, you'll still be cacking yourself about giving the groom's speech on your wedding day. You can do what I did, for various reasons, and refuse point blank, but that brings with it tremendous amounts of stick, resentment and unwelcome confusion over who exactly your wedding is actually for – you and your wife, or your guests. People groan at the thought of speeches, yet they simultaneously maintain that they are the 'point' of weddings. They want to see you being ritually humiliated, with a tear in your eye, and will be very much expecting a humorous and well-balanced ten-minute mixture of gushy adoration for your wife, combined with hilarious, self-admonishing anecdotes that capture the very essence of your being and all that you have achieved since you first made an appearance on the planet.

The pressure is on – to be the funny man and the adoring husband, with quick puns, witty rhetoric and slick delivery all wrapped up in just the right amount of sentimentality to amuse and engage the gathered crowd. Whilst no one would ever dare boo, or leave the room should you fail to deliver (apart from the bride at one wedding I witnessed), you don't want the event to deteriorate into a situation where tables are breaking off into private conversation as you reveal your innermost feelings to the world. You simply must get it right, but rest assured that you will be forgiven an awful lot.

The key to speeches (and although I passed on the opportunity at my own wedding, I have written a fair few for friends) is to keep them light-hearted. No one wants to hear of the trials and tribulations you have both faced to get here – this is a time of celebration and make-believe. For one day, make this the fairy-tale you want it to be. The content of the speech should amuse, but not at the expense of anyone else; if you're going to take the rise out of anyone, then it should be yourself. But not too much, otherwise everyone listening (including the bride) is going to think that the bride has married a complete tosser. And you don't want that!

So, here's the low-down on planning the ultimate (ten-minute) speech:

a: A one-minute introduction, welcoming everyone and

introducing everyone at the top table. (Remember, many of the guests won't know who are the parents of whom, and if there are dads, step-dads, step-mums and children from various marriages, then clarifying this will at least prove that at least you know what the hell's going on!).

b: The two-minute giving of gifts; a chance for everyone to relax and feel appreciated, and for you to feel like the most popular man on the planet as you discharge silver cufflinks to the ushers, bouquets to the bridesmaids, and various other presents to everyone who had a hand in arranging your wedding (which can often mean giving a present to virtually everyone who is at your wedding, which kind of defeats the purpose!).

c: A 30-second praise to the catering, bar and waiting staff for looking after you all so well that day – even if the food was crap, cold and late (you don't want them spitting on the cake).

d: A two-minute anecdotal trip down memory lane outlining how you met your bride and how things progressed to marriage.

e: A one-minute light-hearted quip about joining your new extended family – i.e. the in-laws.

f: A 30-second light-hearted quip about being a moody teenager; and some banter about early career ambitions that changed when you realized a degree in the liberal arts wouldn't automatically lead to a job with NASA.

g: A one-minute pre-emptive strike against the best-man's forthcoming speech, explaining that he is a great man, but finds recalling detail difficult and often imbues the truth with needless creative licence to make himself look better in front of others in order to compensate for having a small penis.

h: A two-minute conclusion which will strike a chord of resonance with the assembled crowd as to how important your wife is in your life; followed by an assurance that your failings as a human being can eventually be overcome, with counselling; how you and your wife are embarking on a new phase of your life journey and how any more emails offering an all-day session in the pub followed by a night out in the local lap-dancing club are probably best not sent any more.

Presenting Gratitude

Yes, it's more expense, but this is worth it. A token gift to those who helped make your special day possible. Obviously budget will dictate what you get for everyone, but there should be a little something presented to the following key personnel: the mothers of the bride and groom, the fathers of the bride and groom, the brothers and sisters, any grandparents present, the best man and the maid of honour, the bridesmaids, the page boys and the best-dressed guest. Incorporate this very public gift of giving within the body of your speech and you'll hardly have to speak at all!

Expenses aside, our own wedding is often the only chance we get to say some very private things to our nearest and dearest, very publicly. When else will you get the opportunity to thank your parents for putting up with your funny ways for so long? (Don't forget they've probably got at least five boxes of your belongings that you still haven't had the chance to move into your new home of six years!) When else can we declare our appreciation for our siblings, despite all those many years of bitter rivalry, fights and arguments? Use your wedding as the ideal opportunity to get everything off your chest that would feel a bit too gushy, and let's face it, a bit too 'gay' to say at any other moment in our lives. Weddings, whether you like it or not, are very sentimental occasions and the setting couldn't be more perfect … On top of that, you might make a few people cry, and that, my friend, is the sign of a very good wedding indeed!

The Best Man's Speech
Once you've done your duty, finally you can sit down at the top table, relieved your speech is over. Your brow is hot, your underarms are sweaty but the speech went well. Surely you can relax now, the worst is over … well, sorry, but now it's his turn. The best man stands up and adjusts his jacket. This is the man responsible for booking the stripper and making you explain to your now wife that the love bite you received in Barcelona on your stag do was merely an accident. And he has carte blanche to do his worst. He's about to stand up and announce to the world that as a twelve-year-old you used to sit on your left hand so that those early wanks felt like there was third-party involvement. He knows you used to have a thing about your Aunty Lara and is about to tell everyone in the room that Uncle Phil has avoided paying income tax for 16 years. He has you by the balls and you know it!

If you can, have a quiet word with your best man, before the day, about what you feel might work well in the speech and what wouldn't. Rhys, in his questionnaire wrote,

'The funniest/best speeches I have heard are those that are made up; comprised of jokes. The most boring are those based solely on "life stories". These are normally only funny to those involved and alienate the rest of the audience. Also, don't be too rude.'

I'm Your Daddy Now...
And then it's the turn of your 'new dad'. You won't have an awful lot of control over the content, but the order of the day is damage limitation. Primarily, the point of the father-of-the-bride speech is the 'letting go' of a daughter to another male of the species. It will pain him, but by now he will have come to realize, if not accept, that you've probably had your wicked way with his daughter, and probably more than once. With this in mind, you'd be wise to approach your father-in-law a few weeks before the wedding and ascertain what it is he plans to say. Most dads will smile cunningly, tap their nose and ignore your request. Smile back, take off your coat and assume the boxing position. If you're not laughed out of the house (or knocked out) you might be invited to an insight into the content of the speech in question. Chances are you won't, but instead will just have to expect the speech will be subtly hostile and know full well that you won't have the opportunity to publicly respond, without making yourself look like an eejit.

Have Your Cake, And Eat It

The wedding cake is an odd thing. The truth of the matter is that most people will eat it and most people will say they like it, but in reality they are enjoying the icing whilst secretly crumbling the fruit content to make it look like it spilt on the plate. It's the turkey-at-Christmas scenario – it looks the part and it's traditional, and therefore everyone feels it would be rude not to have it, but ... bollocks! I hate wedding cake, and my wife will take a sliver, but can take it or leave it. A good friend of ours, Jane, is the epitome of a domestic goddess and insisted on cooking us our 'wedding cake'. The end result was a veritable mountain of

Nigella Lawson's cherry chocolate muffins all individually cased and presented beautifully. They were absolutely divine and they cost nothing (well, they cost us nothing, but I'm sure Jane felt the pinch). The end result was as stunning, if not more so, as any fancy-layered wedding cake. Plus they were unique, and they were lapped up by guests with far more gusto than I've ever seen the second tier of a traditional wedding cake disappear.

There is also something quite unhealthy and worrying about a cake that must 'sit' for weeks, if not months, before it is served – just a basic understanding of bacteria and the chances of an unhygienic storage facility could mean disaster for you and your guests.

Okay, I'm obviously biased and bound to think that all my choices were great. And I admit that cutting a large, perfectly iced cake has a bit more photographic appeal than fifty guests hovering around a tower of muffins unwilling to be the first one to break the symmetry ... but as with all these decisions, it's ultimately what you and your bride want that matters.

Let's Face The Music, And Dance...

There are certain decisions you will make during your wedding preparations that will dictate the tone of the whole event – venue ranks quite highly, as do the dress and the catering on offer. But something that may not appear too important, on first consideration, is the aural appeal of a wedding. Now, thankfully, no one is going to be judging you on your clear, crisp delivery of the wedding vows or your speech. But they will be listening out for the decisions you make regarding the music employed for the day. This music will include everything from the hymns sung at church to the CD tracks played in the registry office and the music selections played by the DJ later on in the evening – of which you are both in control. However, the signature tune is the one you choose to take the floor with when you have your first dance with your new wife ... So what's it going to be? A rock ballad? A song from one of the shows? A boy band? A solo soprano? There's so much to choose from, some of which you really like and some of which you just feel captures the moment, perfectly.

Take your time, buy or download all the CDs you need to make sure your choice is the right one. By all means be soppy, by all means be amusing, by all means be romantic, but make that decision well – at a modern-day 21st-century wedding, you've not only got to worry about the official photographer you've employed, you've also got a room full of guests pointing their mobile phones at you, capturing every second of the dance, in surround sound.

We spent so much time deciding on the tracks suitable for the registry office that we completely forgot about a 'dance floor' song. Luckily my quick-thinking best man, Zazz, was there to make the decision on our behalf, and chose Marillion's 'Kayleigh', in a bid to appeal to our misplaced childhoods. I hope that he was being ironic.

Play That Funky Music, DJ Boy

Some DJs are really good and some are absolutely terrible. It might be that your wedding is the first time you have ever hired a DJ, so you'll have no previous experience of dealing with them and not have a clue, when scanning through the local classifieds, whether the DJ with the coolest name and who has paid for the biggest advert is any better or worse than the two either side of him. It's pot luck – unless you ask to come to an event that the DJ is due to play at before you book.

What you want is a DJ with a selection of everything you like, plus a selection of generic crowd pleasers, and without a '70s mega-mix appearing anywhere in the play list. What you do not want is a DJ who is self-obsessed and who will mumble incessantly throughout the music and scoff at your guests when they request something that is half decent. Get the DJ right, however, and the night will work out a treat. A good tactic is to scan the local bars for DJ nights as soon as your wedding preparations begin, go and hear what's on offer, and if you like what you hear, ask for a card.

Introducing, Live On Stage ...
It seems to me that live music is always the best way to appreciate music. Okay, so it is seldom as finely tuned and polished as recorded music which has benefited from hours of technical work in a mixing studio, but there is something so powerful and moving about raw talent that it is absolutely exhilarating. A band will only play what they know, so you'll have a job getting the Bedford Barbershop Boys to do a rendition of The Prodigy's 'Firestarter', but if you like a certain style, you'll get it, unadulterated, all night, without a DJ coming in, thinking that the *Titanic* theme tune might be a good idea...

If there's anyone musical within the wedding party (especially the bride or groom) then there's an opportunity for them to join in on an instrument or vocals for a one-off cameo appearance. The whole nature of live music, as opposed to recorded music, certainly opens up the possibilities for mass sing-alongs with all of your guests, which would be a fitting end to any wedding reception.

Again, be sure to hear the band play at another venue before hiring them, to make sure their advertising claims truly represent their musical talent. As most bands have a limit, both in terms of material and stamina, to how long they are able to play, sometimes you are able to get the best of both worlds by combining a live band and a DJ so that all tastes are catered for.

The Getaway

And as the evening wears on, and the crowd gets merrier, you suddenly find it's time to start winding up the day and making a move ... and there's no getting away from the fact that some clown is going to tie a load of detritus to the back of your getaway motor. There will be empty cans of beans, balloons, ribbons, bunting, party-popper streamers and slightly damp confetti which will stain the metallic paintwork, get clogged up in the ventilation and play havoc with the wipers if it's raining. Why? Who knows? But do it they will and you'll be expected to grin and thank the bastard. Obviously, if it's a hired car, you won't mind too much, but if it's your motor you'll be cursing them for the entire honeymoon. Unless you particularly like the 'just driven through a toilet paper factory' look, accept your fate, drive about a mile away and then take your trusty penknife and remove the offending articles. If you receive any resistance from your new bride explain the safety aspects – highlighting the fact that because you're obviously newlywed, thieves might be encouraged to break into the car looking for presents and cash ... worked for me.

... And Perform You Will

Thankfully, although you will no doubt be absolutely wasted on your wedding day, there's something instinctive about being able to perform (albeit it probably won't be your finest hour) on your wedding night. Although it is a very grey area of the law, you do have a responsibility to consummate the marriage and although nobody is expecting you to hang the sheets out of the bridal-suite balcony as proof, there is still a pressure on you to resist the urge to fall asleep for the next 14 hours until you have had a chance to enjoy conjugal relations with your wife. Not that this is a particularly stressful prospect; far from it, in fact. And once that final 'job' is done, it really is time now for you to relax...

The Honeymoon

And now for the
fun bit ...

Time, Please, Gentlemen

When organizing our plans for our honeymoon most of us have to book time off work. If any part of your holiday requirement contravenes normal work policy (requesting more than two weeks' holiday in one go, booking time off when another member of staff is on holiday, and so on) thankfully even the most hardened boss is going to find it difficult to refuse, given that this is your *honeymoon* and not just a last-minute holiday booked through Teletext when you came in from the pub. Obviously, the more notice you can give, the easier it is all round to get everything you want, and the less risk there is that you'll put everyone at work's back up. (Not that you care, but it could lead to sour relations when you return.)

Be sure to book as much time off as you can and

allow some time both immediately before and after the actual dates of your wedding/honeymoon. The day before the wedding, for example, will be essential for picking up bits and pieces from the florist/off-licence/caterers/cake makers etc. Equally, on your return from two weeks of non-stop sun, sand and sex, you really don't want to get off the flight knowing that there's nearly 1000 emails waiting for you, at least not without a day at home to mentally prepare yourself for it.

Here Or There?

What's it to be, the secluded island in the Indian Ocean, the whistle-stop tour of major European capital cities or the quiet retreat in the seaside cottage a little closer to home? Choosing the ideal destination is really difficult, and if someone else is paying for it, they may already have booked it and it might not be somewhere either of you were even considering.

At the end of the day, it really doesn't matter, because it's your honeymoon and you're going to love it. From the questionnaires I received when researching this book, the jury was still out on what works and what doesn't. The deserted island was certainly great for 'getting to know each other properly', but if you're both buzzy, social butterflies, then two weeks with only hermit crabs for company can get a bit boring. The city experience can be exciting, fresh, educational and fun, but you might come back exhausted and in need of a holiday! The home-from-home option seemed to come up trumps in that it allowed the couple their private time, but if a bit of third-party stimulus was needed, then it was there on tap, and in a language that was fully understood...

We went to my father-in-law's house in the

Pyrenees with my father-in-law, his family, their dog, their friend from Spain, her two grown-up children and our three-year-old daughter. It was marvellous because it was as unconventional as our wedding had been. (The only downer was me having to finish a book I was working on at the time and our house in the UK being emptied of all our worldly goods by thieves whilst we were away.)

If you do decide to fly away to foreign climes for your honeymoon, then don't forget to mention your new married status. Stephen writes:

'If you're flying off, tell the staff on the check-in desk in a coy and offhand manner. You might get an upgrade and/or champagne.'

That *Time Of The Month*

It would be churlish to mention it to her, and I'm sure she's got it under control, but you'll both, no doubt, be wanting a bit of a sex-fest both on your wedding night and during your honeymoon. The unfortunate timing of a period could seriously put the dampeners on that taking place (unless you're *that* sort of couple). So it might be as well just to double-check it with her first. Just in case she's got so caught up in the wedding whirl that she hasn't worked out her dates in advance. Rest assured that if there is a possible clash, she'll know the tricks of the trade (involving the contraceptive pill and hormonal tablets) that can ensure she will be period-free during your honeymoon. This all needs to be arranged, through your partner's doctor, well in advance of the wedding, and it may mean deliberately causing a shift in her cycle to accommodate your mutual desire for a tampon-free honeymoon. If this is the case, you may have to resort to other methods of contraception for at least a month sometime in the near future. Don't moan; buy some condoms and be thankful she's taking your sexual needs so seriously!

Filling Your Time

Funny as it may sound, when was the last time you spent a week with your fiancée absolutely alone? Come to think of it, when was the last time you spent more than two days with your fiancée, without meeting up with someone else one of you knows, or speaking on the telephone to a friend or family member? Have you ever? Weird, isn't it, but the likelihood is that unless you've been on holiday together to a remote desert island, you haven't actually spent a huge amount of time together, alone as a couple. Just to make matters a little bit more skewed, for the past few months, if not years, the two of you have been intensely involved in planning a wedding together, and that has meant constantly talking to others, meeting with others, whilst also going to work, going out with mates and generally not *actually* seeing that much of each other.

Suddenly, you're booked to spend an uninterrupted fortnight together ... What on earth are you going to do? (Apart from the obvious, but 24 hours of non-stop jiggy will take its toll even on you, you big stud muffin). What on earth are you going to talk about?

It should come as no surprise, therefore, that once the giddy heights of the wedding have faded into fuzzy memories, and once you have passed the first few days of the holiday, and are established in your honeymoon routine of sex, breakfast, sex, beach, sex, lunch, beach, dinner, sex, repeat – after about day four, when neither of you have the energy or willingness to laugh yet again at the best man's comments, or your speech, or that girl's dress, you reach an awkward silence, begin to twiddle your thumbs, hum and look around, hoping that an entourage from the wedding is in fact hiding behind the next palm tree just waiting for the chance to pop out and say hello.

Your perfect honeymoon suddenly feels a little less fun, with no movies, mobiles, email or possibly even a telly to distract you; in fact it could quickly start to become one of the most unpleasant holidays of your life. To make matters worse you might even end up having a huge argument over who left the loo seat up, *again* ... and then it clicks. Other than your birth (which you can't remember), moving house (for which you have solicitors to scream at), and dying (which is yet to happen, and again, you won't remember), there is nothing more stressful than getting married. The two of you are as wound-up as tightly-sprung coils and although you've been denying it, the last few months have battered you both, emotionally and physically. But you are married now, and you just both need to remember how to relax again. Only when you stop stressing and really start to relax will the true smiles begin to appear, and it is then that the sex gets even better and, pity your little fella, gets even more constant.

First Married Row

Believe it or not, you may well have your first married row on your honeymoon – don't worry, you're both still stressed from the wedding and it's going to take a while yet to unwind. You're also probably in a foreign country, or even in a part of Britain that you are unfamiliar with, which can be stressful in its own right. Anyway, you are going to have lots of arguments, as a married couple, over the years, so getting the first one over with early on is probably a good thing.

No doubt the reason for the argument will be minor and, before the afternoon has finished, normal service will be resumed.

Yeah, Cheers, It's Lovely ...

On your return you have some final duties to attend to. Whether you like what they got you or hate it, it is common courtesy to say thanks for all the presents you got for your wedding. It is at this moment you really wish that you'd kept a record, and it is at this moment that your wife reveals that she did. Don't you just love her to bits! So on the ball.

Anyway, you're not ungrateful, but for some reason the prospect of writing thank-you notes for all those wedding presents is a bit too reminiscent of your mum making you write thank-you notes to grandparents for all those horrific jumpers you got as a little boy. We clam up, come over all queer, and generally avoid the point as long as humanly possible. Thank-you notes aren't there to rub in how generous your friends and family have been. Far from it, bearing in mind that as most people probably bought you an item from your wedding list which was then mailed to you, the chances are they never actually set eyes on the item – it was ordered at a till, or online, and paid for – that's it. They just have to assume that the company really did send the right item, to the right address, on time. Your thank-you note is their receipt – proof of delivery and proof that the mail order chap in the John Lewis warehouse didn't decide to exchange the Waterford crystal wine goblet your mate paid for, with a pair of his nan's false teeth.

On every note be sure to specify the item you are thanking the person for and put in a line to say how wonderful it is. Hopefully, like me, you have appalling handwriting and no self-respecting wife in the world is going to want you to scrawl anything on those posh thank-you notes. Result.

Lights Down, Stage Left ...
Welcome To Married Life!

It might be during the honeymoon or it might be months after married life has truly begun, but you suddenly realize that the wedding is over. Really over. You are married and have been now for some time. It really happened and everything is still great. You made the right decision and life continues to be really good fun. The last few months have been stressful and hard work, but it's all gone without a hitch and, hey, you've been married for a while and you're still talking to one another. How cool is that? Another chapter in your life is now closed, and as you are now the world's expert on weddings you are going to be offering advice to those who follow in your footsteps for years to come. Of course, as the sort of chap you are, you'll understand if they ask you politely to bugger off so that they can make their own mistakes...

If Things Go Wrong

Oh *@£%*@$!!!

No one wants to think about a relationship stalling just when it should be taking flight. If this has happened to you, then it could be the preparations for the wedding that have driven you both to the point of distraction – you are planning the most important day of your lives and yet you are emotionally careering away from each other in the process. Everyone gets stressed about a wedding, not least the two people that it affects the most. There are times when you think that everyone is making such a big deal out of it, you're suddenly not sure if it's what you want to do. You've seen your fiancée's mood swing like a pendulum for many a month now and she's not the same carefree bundle of laughs she was when you were just dating or living together. In fairness, you might not have been a huge bundle of laughs either yourself. And relations with your in-laws and your own family may be at breaking point.

Communication, as always, is the simple answer to many of these problems. But most importantly it has to be communication between the two of you, not moaning about the other to a third-party. That's not going to help at all.

A quick solution is to slow everything down, take stock of the situation and realize that whatever plans you still have to make, they will get sorted in time. Undoubtedly what is lacking is some 'you two' time, time together which you put on the backburner because you have so many suppliers, friends and well-wishers fighting for attention. If this is the case, then declare one day of the week to be 'non-wedding-related'; this is where you remember who you are – a couple very much in love. You could spend this day on a meal out or a trip to the cinema or just watching trashy telly together instead of spending even longer surfing the net for dress designs and anything else wedding-related.

Looking Elsewhere For Comfort

The preparations may have turned your fiancée into a wedding-obsessed monster who is so stressed about the event that she is no longer recognizable. In fairness, the wedding may be having a negative effect on you too; you may have become distant and irritable, and the two of you may have reached a stage where you simply can't talk to each other about anything *but* the wedding. Suddenly you become resentful about the whole process; everything was so much easier when you were just boyfriend and girlfriend, or living together, or partners. Suddenly, the pressure of the wedding is showing through and altering your very characters. Suddenly you and/or your fiancée aren't that pleasant to be around ... and suddenly you're out with your mates on a rare night of fun and you're looking around at the totty on offer. Stop. Go home immediately. Or change venues. You do love your fiancée, deeply, but you might momentarily forget that, in the heat of your current emotions, and make a terrible, terrible mistake. Leave the single life behind. You're engaged now.

Weddings are stressful, but seeking solace in another woman's pants isn't the fix-all it might appear as you stagger around a nightclub spilling your pint of Stella. Go home and take a shower. When you've rid your mind and body of impure thoughts, lie beside your sleeping partner and look closely at her still form. This is the woman who will wipe your arse in years to come, when you are no longer capable. This is the woman who will be the mother to your children and will probably wash your socks for the next 50 or so years. This is the woman YOU asked to marry you. Now, take a deep breath, put the whole unsavoury experience behind you, and start working out which CDs and DVDs you could flog on eBay to raise a bit more cash.

If The Damage Is Done

Sometimes you just have to come to the conclusion that you no longer wish to go ahead with the wedding, or even the relationship. This can feel like a monumental thing to do, but it would be so much worse to continue with the wedding regardless. It is possible to delay a wedding, and it may be that buying that extra time is all that you need to fix whatever the problem(s) might be. It might be that no delay in the world is going to help; you just don't work together any more. Fine. Just let her know immediately and all those involved as soon as you can. Cancelling a wedding is bound to be embarrassing and there will inevitably have been expenses lost, but these are minor problems compared to going into a marriage that you know is destined to fail before you celebrate your first wedding anniversary.

It would be rude to keep hold of any presents you may have already received for the engagement or wedding and you'd be churlish to request the ring back. Though if you're the one doing the breaking up, then it will probably be thrown at your head anyway.

It is ultimately an honourable thing to break off an engagement if the relationship has failed, but that is not to say everyone involved, especially the bride, will think you are an honourable person. Learn from the experience and maybe apply a little more caution the next time you think that you're in love with someone.

But Before You Do Anything Rash...

There are organizations out there to help couples in trouble, whether you are married or not. Some are free and some cost money, but they are all there to help. If you can overcome your prehistoric prejudices regarding how useful 'a middle-aged lesbian counsellor who's never been laid' (for there are no others, in your mind) can possibly be, and how much she could help you in your particular situation, then you will probably be pleasantly surprised. And the experience may really help the two of you understand what your differences are and begin to work them out.

Relate (*see contact details at the end of the book*) would be a great place to start. Whether or not their service is likely to work for you is completely dependent on whether the two of you *want* it to work. You both need to commit to turning up to the sessions together and keeping an open mind. If one or both of you can't make the time and effort for a half-hour lifeline to your relationship, then you really shouldn't be pretending to be in a relationship at all.

Afterword

By now, your wedding may well be just a distant memory forever etched on your mind. Or it might, of course, still need to take place and you've rushed through to this page prematurely (not the first time, hey, mate?). But either way, you've got through it: emotionally, psychologically and metaphysically. Amazing. There you were, not two months ago, wondering if the DJ would play 'Smack My Bitch Up' as you took your wife on the dance floor for the very first time ... and look at you now, with the log fire blazing away, romantically sharing a bottle of red wine as the remnants of an incredibly tasty take-away lie forgotten and rejected on the low coffee table...

All the presents are now opened, and you've found a home for the umpteen picture frames, vases and glass bowls you received. This marriage lark, it turns out, is a complete walk in the park. For once you're not going to worry about whether the mango chutney is going to stain your deep shag-pile carpet, or how you'll manage to get the glass ring-marks off your new laminated floor. And why aren't you going to worry about them? Well, first you're still high on the glow of marriage and things simply couldn't get any better, and second your wife has just declared she's eight weeks late ... and that, my friend, means a whole new experience and, funnily enough, a whole new book to buy...

Useful Contacts

There are both good and bad sources of information available on the Internet. It is important to research as many sites as possible and to try and get a real feel for an organization or service before you commit. The Internet is a constantly changing phenomenon and therefore good and bad sites are forever popping up and dropping off. There follows a list, in my opinion, of useful websites, where you can find out more about issues raised in this book. All links and contact details were checked at the time of going to press.

General

Family Planning Association
020 7837 4044
www.fpa.org.uk

Relate
0845 130 4016
www.relate.org.uk

Register Offices

Registrar General (England)
Marriages Section
General Register Office
Smedley Hydro
Trafalgar Road
Birkdale
Southport
PR8 2HH
01704 569824
www.gro.gov.uk

Registrar General (Wales)
Marriages Section
General Register Office
Smedley Hydro
Trafalgar Road
Birkdale
Southport
PR8 2HH
01704 569824
www.gro.gov.uk

General Register Office (Northern Ireland)
Registrar General
Oxford House
49–55 Chichester Street
Belfast
BT1 4HL
028 9025 2028
www.groni.gov.uk

General Register Office for Scotland
New Register House
Edinburgh
EH1 3YT
0131 334 0380
www.gro-scotland.gov.uk

Financial Products

www.moneysupermarket.com

Tour Operators

Thomas Cook Weddings – 01733 418450
Kuoni International Weddings – 01306 747007
Virgin Weddings – 01293 744265

Wedding Websites

www.confetti.co.uk
www.hitched.co.uk
www.weddingguide.co.uk
www.weddings.co.uk
www.dianeandvincent.com

Gifts For The Groom

www.amazon.co.uk
www.firebox.com
astore.amazon.co.uk/pestleandmort-21/detail/140190288X

Also by Jon Smith:

For Adults (18–80)
The Bloke's Guide To Pregnancy
The Bloke's 100 Top Tips For Surviving Pregnancy
The Bloke's Guide To Baby Gadgets
Websites That Work
Smarter Business Start Ups

For Children (8–12)
Toytopia

References

1. Elizabeth Cashdan (1998) Women's mating strategies. *Evolutionary Anthropology: Issues, News and Reviews* 5(4), 134-143.

2. L.R. Hiatt (1984) Your mother-in-law is poison. *Man*, 19 (June), 183-198.

Hay House Titles of Related Interest

Bloke's Guide to Surviving Pregnancy, by Jon Smith

Dr Lucy Atcheson's Guide to Perfect Relationships,
by Dr Lucy Atcheson

You Can Have What You Want, by Michael Neill

The Law of Attraction, by Esther and Jerry Hicks

Love Yourself ... and It Doesn't Matter Who You Marry!,
by Eva-Maria Zurhurst